Cooperative Adoption™

A Handbook

By
Mary Jo Rillera
and
Sharon Kaplan

TRIADOPTION® Publications
Westminster, California

Thank You To:
Carole Land, Steve Rillera, Diane Leach, Bonnie Endo and Pat Sanders for editing assistance.
Barry Slobin, Martin Brandfon and Ron Regev for photographs.
Jon Ryan and Concerned United Birthparents for running the typesetting.
Kathy Sly for resumes and suggestions.
Vikki Schummer for sample authorizations.
The Cooperative Adoption Support Group.
and ... the families who contributed their stories.

Published by
TRIADOPTION Publications
TRIADOPTION Library, Inc.
P. O. Box 638
Westminster, CA 92684

ISBN: 0-941770-03-6

May 1984, 1st Edition
July 1985, 2nd Edition

***DEDICATED TO** those who love potential and possibilities.*

Contents

SECTION I: PREPARING

SECTION II: DOING

SECTION III: DOCUMENTING

SECTION IV: COOPERATIVE FAMILIES

SECTION I

PREPARING

Understanding Cooperative Adoption

Cooperative adoption represents possibilities. It is used by each participant differently. Cooperative adoption adds options and extends family relationships. Cooperative adoption is knowing that children all come into this life whole, with all rights and relationships intact. And it is understanding that no one has the right to interrupt those rights or deprive another being of them.

Cooperative adoption is the child's access to both families, to both sets of parents, with progressive participation in the decisions that will affect his/her life. It is important to view adoption from the child's perspective rather than from the adults' perspective. If the child has access to both families, (s)he does not lose anything, and both sets of parents, by the nature of the arrangement will have continued access to each other.

In the past, birthfamilies and adoptive families were considered to have antagonistic interests. Somehow the fact that they were all human beings with a child's interest at heart got lost. It doesn't matter how this happened and there is no blame. What matters now is that adoption ADDS OPTIONS to the child's life and to the lives of all relatives. The ideal adoption expands the child's life experiences. The ideal adoption is cooperative participation and interaction between all birth and adoptive family members. In the ideal adoption the child loses nothing ... not relationships, not knowledge, not continuity, not identity, not birthfamily, not siblings, not grandparents, not parents, not one single thing! Instead (s)he gains relationships, knowledge, continuity, identity, security, parents, siblings, grandparents, etc.

Secrecy and loss have made traditional adoptions difficult. Cooperative adoption is a positive option, a chance for everyone to celebrate, and a chance for everyone to gain.

Cooperative adoption requires an understanding that all relationships are continually renegotiable. None of us stay the same and all our dreams, needs and relationships change with time, maturity and experience. In a cooperative adoption the child must be seen as having progressiive participation in his/her own life and in the relationships established by adoption. It acknowledges that the unconsulted party, the adoptee, maintains control of self. With this in mind it is easier for the adults to view themselves as guardians of the child's future and to acknowledge the great gift they have all gained in creating and nurturing a life.

What you will find in this book is a step-by-step guide to understanding the alternatives available. It is a handbook for avoiding adversary adoptions and facilitating cooperative adoptions.

Feelings of anxiety, disbelief, discomfort and excitement may surface as you read through this book. Remember that everyone has multiple emotions about most things. There is no rule that says you must only feel one thing at one time. You are allowed to work through your feelings as you choose and to feel anything you choose. It is not unusual to find that an open process such as cooperative adoption will feel uncomfortable for some of you. Know that this is not different from the emotional process for any important, identity-related relationship. People must learn to love and trust each other in any meaningful relationship.

Just as divorce once left its participants unable to relate, so has adoption. Just as divorce has moved in possibilities from adversary to cooperative, so can adoption. As part of a transition, cooperative adoption participants are traveling footpaths rather than paved highways. They may seem unfamiliar. They may seem untraveled. But that does not make the highway better. There would be no highways if footpaths and buggy paths had not preceded them.

Cooperative adoption is what you make it. It is continually evolving and you may find that the harder you try to define it the broader the definition becomes.

Cooperative adoption takes seeing each participant as whole unto themselves, coming together as many whole people to extend a family rather than as pieces to create a whole.

The following definitions may be helpful as you proceed.

ADOPTIVE FAMILY: Family not genetically related who have become the legal guardians of a child. Custodial family.

ADVERSARY ADOPTION: A legal transfer of custody and responsibility of a child during minority years where the birth and adoptive families do not personally negotiate. An adoption in which the child is not seen as a progressive participant.

AGENCY ADOPTION: One coordinated by a licensed social service agency.

BIRTHFAMILY: Family genetically related who no longer has legal guardianship of their child. Non-custodial family.

BY RELATIVE ADOPTION: An adoption that takes place within a family structure. (Step-parent adoptions fall in this category but are discussed as a separate definition). It could be that the grandparents, aunts, uncles, brothers or sisters take over the care of the child. Often this is done informally with the child always knowing about his/her birthparents. At other times this care is formalized into transfer of guardianship by a legal adoption, and in some cases, the child is kept from the truth about his/her birth and relationships.

COOPERATIVE ADOPTION: The child is continuously considered a primary participatory partner even when still unable to speak for his/her self, so that as the child grows, (s)he will become an increasingly involved participant in the decisions that affect his/her life. The birth and adoptive families continue interaction and personal communication about their concerns. There is a legal transfer of responsibility for the child during his/her minority years.

CUSTODIAL FAMILY: The primary nurturing family.

FERTILIZATION ADOPTION: Artificial insemination, surrogate, embryo transplant, and in-vitro fertilization involve the utilization of donated sperm and/or eggs to create a new life. In all instances this involves a formal or informal custody transfer, by virtue of the fact that the child will be raised by at least one parent to whom (s)he is not genetically related.

FOSTER ADOPTION: One in which persons who have served as foster parents to a child for any period of time, either formally or informally, assume permanent custody by finalizing an adoption.

GRANDPARENTING: A formal or informal arrangement where an older, more secure couple or single party take in both the young parent and her newborn or yet unborn child. This expands the options for all involved by establishing expanded relationships.

GREY/BLACK MARKET ADOPTION: Buying or selling of children. Not done by legally sanctioned methods. Anytime a profit is being made by someone while transferring custody of a child other than payment for direct medical expenses and appropriate legal fees, there may be questionable practices involved.

GUARDIANSHIP: A legal transfer of custody, responsibility and decision making to a guardian approved by the court. In this process court records are not "sealed", and the child's birth certificate is not altered. Guardianship allows for increasing consideration of the child's desires as (s)he matures. (Some schools of thought hold that this legal state would be adequate to provide all necessary permanence and care for children without taking away any of their legal rights or relationships).

INDEPENDENT/PRIVATE ADOPTION: An adoption arranged privately between the birthparent(s) and adoptive parent(s). Often facilitated by a doctor, lawyer or other party not associated with a licensed adoption agency.

STEP-PARENT ADOPTIONS: Technically step-parent adoptions are considered to be "by relative" adoptions and involve termination of one parent's rights with a subsequent spouse deciding to formally take permanent custody and responsibility for another's child(ren). Often includes a change of surname but not a change of given names.

Children's Rights

The basic premise of cooperative adoption is that the child has access to both families, and is a progressive participant in the decisions that affect his/her life and relationships. This access is not limited to written or described information which would make up only a small portion of learning tools, but includes visual, verbal, and physical access as well.

To understand cooperative adoption one must see children as people not possessions. Children are adults in training.

There is no magic age where people suddenly acquire rights. Human rights must apply to people of any age even though some rights may seem inappropriate because the infant or toddler is temporarily unable to exercise rights. Society should work harder to guarantee the protection of the rights of those who cannot protect themselves. If rights are not acknowledged as a natural part of every person's life it is difficult to grow up understanding and expecting them. The idea of children having the same rules and guidelines as adults uncovers many fears and anxieties in those who feel it is their job to protect and control children. This type of concern is used as a barrier to children achieving self-determination. Self-determination is a fundamental principle on which all other discussion of rights is built.

A child's potential cannot be assessed when they are viewed as helpless or are deprived of their self-determination. Our society often views children as useless except in relation to adult needs. When children were a financial asset to a family, because they helped with chores and necessities of survival, there was self-determination inherent in the parent-child relationship. Children were participants in their daily lives even as toddlers. Today, children are often considered a financial liability, and that may be why we have developed a double standard. One set of morals and behavior is acceptable for adults and the same set is unacceptable for children. No wonder children have difficulty deciphering what is appropriate and acceptable behavior or emotional reaction.

Children become good adults by practicing. They learn from observation and mimicry, which makes a "do as I say not as I do" attitude uninterpretable to them.

The goal of children's rights is to improve family life not destroy it; to make children useful not helpless; to enhance the adult world not diminish it; and to liberate parents not make them wardens.

The fundamental inequality of a child is simply that (s)he is a child. There is a tendency in our civilization to keep our kids weak, innocent, helpless and dependent. At times we indoctrinate, patronize, ignore, dominate, prohibit, coerce, belittle and manipulate them. Often we deny them the opportunity for self-determination, economic independence, political power, sexual experience, self-education, self-discovery and justice. After we discriminate against them in so many ways we have the audacity to express concern over their developing a healthy identity, a positive self-image, independence or self-worth.

Children are often placed in a position where they are victims of a social system over which they have little or no control or influence. Adoption in any form places children in a victimized position. We are surrounded with professionals who purport to be devoting their lives and careers to helping children but in fact may perpetrate oppression, exploitation and helplessness. Much of conventional 20th century adoption takes away a child's right to self-determination.

Children learn helplessness because it is expected of them. In presuming that children cannot take progressive responsibility and become progressive participants in decisions that affect them, we teach them that they are not capable.

Because many parents who consider placing their children in an adoptive home are young themselves, they too are seen as helpless, unfit and incapable. The adults in their lives often describe to these young parents all that they cannot do instead of nurturing their capabilities. People learn to parent. Young people can learn to parent too. They are not automatically incapable of coping with parenthood and financial responsibility simply because they are young or have no previous experience or track record.

There are some adults who may see children's rights, children's self-determination and progressive participation as impractical or impossible. These adults should attempt to see children as partners in life, much the same as a marriage, friendship and a family are partnerships. All parties can acknowledge each other's right to self-determination and concurrent participation. We have developed a generation of adopted individuals who are still being treated by society as non-participants in self-determination about their lives or relationships. No matter what their age the courts, states and agencies refuse to give these individuals vital information about themselves basing the refusal on other's "rights". The adoptee's individual rights are never seen exclusively, but only in the shadow of the rights of the adults involved.

What rights? Many adoptees grow up with limited information about their genetic histories, medical histories, physical characteristics and development patterns. They had no participation in the decision to be shifted from one family to another or to have their records "sealed". And they remain bound by these decisions and must live without knowledge, without access to files and records, without relationships; to which they might choose access given the opportunity. Because some adults may not be curious or want to know more does not mean all adoptees will not be curious. Under the guise of "protection" adoptees have more birth certificates than other citizens, more parents than most other citizens, more names than other citizens, and more records sealed in courts, agencies and state departments than other citizens. These "special privileges" enslave and encumber adoptees. Given equal privilege, equal rights, equal justice and equal responsibility, adoptees would regain their right to self-determination.

The argument that few contemporary children have the right to self-determination is moot. Children without self-determination become dependent adults. The families in cooperative adoptions can be superb examples of progressive parenting by practicing self-determination with their children and with each other. All family members can establish permanent areas of participation and self-worth when they have an identity that they have participated in developing and defining.

Basically, children's rights are everyone's rights. We were all children and we continue through our children. There is no greater pleasure than observing the accomplishment of another with the knowledge that you were a supporting, nurturing adjunct. We cannot take credit for what any other human being accomplishes but we can take credit for what we have given that the person (knowingly or unknowingly) has utilized. When a flower blooms we seldom recall the fertilizer, or the water, or the soil, or the time, or the attention that was necessary. We can quietly observe its beauty, never claiming its beauty for our own. If we can nurture our children as unselfishly as that we will have done a good job.

Being Whole

One of the most valuable tools for preparing to expand relationships and family is to view yourself and all other participants as whole. People are all born whole, intact unto themselves. People remain whole throughout life.

It is not uncommon to talk with persons involved in traditional adoptions who will express that they never viewed the other participants in their extended family as whole. Birthparents may not view themselves as whole without their child, or their child as whole without the birth family. Adoptees may not view themselves as whole without their birth family connections, or either set of parents as whole without the adoptee in their lives. Adoptive parents may not view themselves as whole without a child, the adoptee as whole without them, or the birthparent as whole without the child.

Childlessness, infertility and surrender all are seen by society as incomplete ... as unwhole. Lack of feeling whole is not unique to adoption, it is rampant in our society.

Don't we need other people? Of course, we do! Relationships enhance our lives. But relationships are better when all participants see themselves as intact rather than desperately needing others to fill their gaps.

How can we feel whole if we are missing something? You can never be missing you. You are always there. Desiring what others have or what we see outside ourselves is common. Think for a moment if acquiring those things has ever made you feel more whole. Usually attaining more money, belongings, friends, understanding, compassion, patience, health, physical strength, etc. adds aspects to our life but does not really touch our core self. If we view wholeness as the place where we are at peace we can see that this comes from inside rather than outside.

This book is not a lesson in wholeness, faith or growth but it does recognize that cooperative adoption works best for those people who see themselves and all others, including the child, as whole.

How can you learn to feel whole if you don't now? We have included a simple visualization exercise to help you with this process. There are many meditations, disciplines and exercises that can increase your awareness of your own wholeness. (See Appendix).

WHOLENESS VISUALIZATION

Sit or lie comfortably, close your eyes, relax, breath evenly and deeply. Imagine you are in the most beautiful garden. It can be a wild garden, an english garden, a backyard garden whatever you want it to be, but it is the most beautiful garden you have ever seen. Walk through the garden, look closely at the colors, smell the flowers, touch the earth and the leaves. Feel the growth, the life all around you. Know that you are as whole, healthy and alive as all that surrounds you.

Now see a younger you, or a you from your past, a you that you thought was unwhole. Forgive that you. Put your arms around that you and see that you as whole.

Invite others into your garden. These can be people from your past or as they are in the present, it can even be an unborn child. Sit and talk with them. Ask them anything you wish, wait a moment for their answers. Tell them anything you want to tell them. Forgive them. See their growth, their life and their wholeness. Show them yours.

When you are ready, slowly open your eyes. Remember, you can return to your garden whenever you want. It is where you recognize wholeness.

Straight Thinking

In the process of establishing a cooperative adoption, it is common for the participants to feel nervous, worry about acceptance/rejection, success or failure. The birthparents may wonder if the prospective adoptive parents will accept them and their baby for placement. The prospective adoptive parents worry about whether the birthparents will like them enough to choose them to raise the child. The child, if an infant or toddler, may not be able to have input in this process, but is the primary reason for the relationship. When the birth and adoptive parents think in terms of the child's needs and questions, the tension is lessened. Many parents state they don't want an ongoing relationship. But the child IS the relationship.

What will the child want to know about both families, in terms of the present or future of his/her life? Don't forget that each child has two sides to his/her birthfamily - the birthmother's and the birthfather's. Many children are more like their fathers, so don't cheat the child by minimizing the birthfather's importance.

The following are some guidelines to help you think about the child's needs.

1. What would you like to know about these people with whom you are becoming close.?

2. If you had just met a couple who had adopted, what questions would enter your mind as to why they adopted and what they knew about the child and the child's background?

3. If you had just met a birthmother or birthfather who had placed their child, what questions would enter your mind as to why they placed their child in an adoptive home and what they knew about the adoptive parents?

4. What was important for you to know about yourself when you were growing up?

5. If the information had not been available to you, how would that have been troublesome to you?

6. At what times in your life has knowledge of your history been important to you? (For instance - filling out doctor's forms, doing family trees in school, filling out background information for college entrance, identifying your mother's maiden name for a bank).

7. If you didn't have the information that you needed to know about yourself, how would you fill in those spaces or get that information? Would you fantasize, use denial of its importance, lie, ask questions, or do research?

Signs Of Readiness

READINESS

Readiness should be a primary concern for ALL parents, for readiness to be a parent affects how we bond to our children, discipline them, and help them get ready to individuate from us and spring into adulthood. The primary concern for prospective birthparents should be that they have dealt thoroughly with their abilities and desires concerning parenting. The primary concern for prospective adoptive parents should be that they have dealt thoroughly with infertility. Readiness for adoption involves a grief process which can take several months or years to complete. Each person completes the process in his/her own style and time. It would be wise to grieve for the children you cannot bear and/or raise yourself before you enter into an adoption arrangement. Adoption is not a cure for infertility or pregnancy. Though it is not entirely possible to thoroughly understand and resolve your feelings before hand it is advisable to, at the very least, look directly at those issues and feelings and acknowledge that what you may not experience now could arise in the future.

For prospective adoptive and birth parents grief includes:

*The stages of grief are outlined by Elizabeth Kubler-Ross in her book *On Death and Dying*.

ADOPTIVE PARENTS

DENIAL: Denial includes not looking at the fact that you cannot produce your own genetic children. It is a feeling of "We don't talk about it" and "Adoption is just like...so it's okay".

ANGER: Anger can take the form of being angry at yourself, your spouse, doctors, attorneys, agencies, or God. It is a time when we need closeness but actually push people away. It is not a good time to try to bond to a child. Don't adopt during this phase.

BARGAINING: This is the time when we say, "Maybe if we switch sides of the bed...", "Maybe if we go on a vacation...", "Maybe if we switch doctors...", "Maybe if we adopt...", ..."THEN MAYBE we'll get pregnant!" There is some desperation behind these "maybes". Bargaining usually goes on in the privacy of your own thoughts.

DEPRESSION: This is a helpless, vulnerable stage where guilt and shame are often experienced because of infertility issues. There may be specific physical responses, such as eating or sleeping difficulties, or generally not feeling well.

ACCEPTANCE: At this stage you regain some mastery over your feelings. You can talk about infertility and can tell people you want to adopt because you are infertile.

BIRTHPARENTS

DENIAL: Not confronting the fact that you are pregnant, that you will not have your baby to hold, nurse, or nurture. It is pretending that you can go on with your life, "put this behind you", and "forget". It is not being able to talk about it. It is acting as though it weren't real.

ANGER: You can be angry at the other birthparent, your parents, birth control, God or yourself. You need to be close to others, yet your anger pushes them further away. Don't surrender your child during this phase. Anger is just feeling out of control and not yet seeing alternatives.

BARGAINING: This is the time when you think, "Maybe if I go along with what others want...", "Maybe if I'm nicer to the other birthparent...", "Maybe if I make God a promise...", "Maybe if I hold my breath..."; ..."THEN MAYBE I'll find out I'm not pregnant or I don't have to relinquish my baby or someone will take care of us." Bargaining is a desperate time of looking for ways out of the situation.

DEPRESSION: This is a time when guilt, shame, and helplessness are often experienced. Each person experiences emotional lows differently. Depression can manifest itself physically in unusual energy patterns. (e.g. sleeping more than usual).

ACCEPTANCE: This is the stage where you regain some sense of control over your feelings. You can talk about your child, the other people involved and the adoption. You have an internal sense of calm.

Feelings of grief can surface over and over again, but hopefully, as time goes on, with less intensity. Some people re-experience their grief at the time of placement, the time the adoption is finalized, or years later when their natural child-bearing years are coming to an end. For birthparents, the birth of or inability to have subsequent children can cause grief-related feelings. For adoptive parents there are many reminders that the children they raise and love have not made them fertile.

Do not use adoption as a replacement of a child you have lost without time to grieve. This includes never being able to get pregnant, stillborns, miscarriages, incomplete adoption, children's deaths and secondary infertility. Remember grief can bring growth. There are excellent books to read about infertility, death, loss and grief. Organizations are available to assist you in moving through this process. Two national resources are:

Concerned United Birthparents
595 Central Avenue
Dover, NH 03820
(603) 749-3744

Resolve Infertility
Box 474
Belmont, MA 02178
(617) 484-2424

SIGNS OF READINESS TO ADOPT FOR PROSPECTIVE ADOPTIVE AND BIRTH PARENTS ARE:

1. Going public with your plan is a sign that you are comfortable with the idea.

2. Doing something about adoption, such as investigating your options, reading books, and joining support organizations.

3. Fantasizing about being an adoptive parent by looking at baby clothes, furniture, and thinking of names. Or about being a non-custodial parent by imagining no longer being pregnant, being without the child and the baby, clothes, etc. being with the adoptive family you have chosen.

4. Being able to admit that adoption is second choice, and there is nothing wrong with that as an option.

5. Recognizing that adoptive parenting and birthparenting are not the same and that everyone gains and loses, and acquires additional tasks and emotions.

6. Mutually agreeing that adoption is your choice and the timing is right for both of you.

7. Being able to love (even if you don't like everything about) the child's other parents and accept that family.

8. Honestly evaluating the financial aspects.

9. Carefully exploring the sexual, racial, religious, age, and medical issues that will be part of this child, and evaluate how these impact you and your family.

10. Thinking about what you expect from the child and what you hope to be giving.

11. Age progressing the child in your mind so you have a clear picture that (s)he will not remain an infant but will become a toddler, teen and adult.

SPECIFIC READINESS SIGNS FOR BIRTHPARENTS:

You May Be Ready If...

a. Your lifestyle is not accommodating to children and you are unable/unwilling to change it at this time.

b. You do not possess parenting tools and are unable/unwilling to learn them at this time.

c. You do not have quality time to spend with your child.

d. You are making this decision yourself, not to please others. You are not trying to get back at or get even with anyone.

e. You are not depending on being able to have subsequent children. (According to a Concerned United Birthparents study 38% of birthparents who surrender do not have other children).

f. You feel responsible and are not trying to avoid dealing with the fact that you are a parent even though that may soon mean you are a non-custodial parent.

g. You acknowledge your child's progressive right to make decisions about his/her relationships as (s)he matures.

h. You like yourself! You have a sense of humor!

SPECIFIC READINESS SIGNS FOR ADOPTIVE PARENTS

You May Be Ready If...

a. Your lifestyle accomodates children. Parenting should be a joy, not a duty.

b. You view a child as an asset, not a liability.

c. If you are married, your marriage is strong and you have similar ideas on child raising and are able to compromise.

d. You have time to share with your child.

e. You do not feel that having children is an automatic necessity of life.

f. You are not embarrassed at not giving birth to children.

g. You are not adopting because you have problems in your marriage or to fill an empty life. Your life needs to be full so you have plenty to give the child.

h. You like yourselves! You have a sense of humor.

Remember, ALL parenting is for a lifetime. Decisions should be made without outside pressures taking precedence. Ideally, they are made with preparation, thought, reflection, caring, love and enough information to make an informed choice. For birthparents, readiness to relinquish the child is not just non-readiness to parent. For adoptive parents, readiness to adopt is not just non-readiness to accept infertility. For both sets of parents, adoption is an option for the child, not a solution to parental problems.

Fear Of Openness

Many people recognize the value of cooperative adoptions intellectually, but some are fearful of the concept on an emotional level.

COMMON FEARS

1. *"I don't want to share my parenting, I don't want to feel like a babysitter, and I don't want to co-parent", say some adoptive parents. "I don't want to be severed from my child, I don't want to feel unwanted/unwelcome, and I don't want my child to be a possession", say some birthparents.*

   The solution is simple really. The birthparent chooses not to be the custodial parent and the adoptive parent chooses to be the custodial parent. The adoptive parent becomes the legal guardian. Children will know who is in charge. You must all feel entitled to a relationship with the child and must determine between yourselves where you will set your parameters.

2. *"The birthparent/adoptive parent might be crazy, abusive or get divorced and do my child harm."*

   Truly "crazy" parents cannot sign legal documents. If you meet each other you can decide how YOU feel. If your fears continue and seem realistic, perhaps you should not proceed with this placement.

3. *"The other parents could change their minds. I could have more grief."*

   We usually gain more than we lose when we risk. Remember what our grandmas told us - "Nothing ventured, nothing gained". Grief hurts, but each time we can grow and gain something as well.

4. *"If we have an open adoption it won't be "as if" the child were born to us.*

   This fear is very much related to the grief process and fertility loss. An adoptive parent can be the parenting and legal parent but never the genetic parent to this child. No children belong to us. Adoptive children aren't your children in the same way as birth children and that's reality! One is not better than the other, they are just different.

5. *"The other parents' lifestyles and values are so different from ours that we don't know how to relate."*

   If you don't like the other parents you might not be able to like the child. Parents and children can be reflections of each other.

6. *"I might like the birthparent so much that I won't want to take away the child." "I might like the adoptive parents so much that I will want to see them all the time and my presence might take away from their relationship with our child.*

   These are entitlement issues. Who will feel entitled to parent the child? Think of it not as taking away but rather giving to the child. All parents involved have control in this negotiating and decision making process.

7. *"I might get so close to the other parents that I will be afraid to lose them as friends".*

   Some prospective mothers have shared that they develop a reciprocal relationship with the birthmother being the adoptive mother's fertile self, and the adoptive mother being the birthmother's infertile self. Why not think of the birth/adoptive parent as a special friend...your best friend. It seems unfamiliar but others have done it sucessfully.

8. *"What if our child wants to go live with the birthfamily?"*

   All relationships are constantly renegotiated. We always need to reevaluate what is best for our children at different stages of their lives. No child stays with us forever. If you have had a good, close relationship with the other family and have learned to like each other, you will begin to think of them as a trustworthy support system for your child. Remember, if parents can love more than one child, then children can love more than one set of parents.

Remember, we don't gain if we don't risk. You can also pull back from your risks because you do have control in your life.

Focus on the adoptee's needs. Cooperative adoption can cut down on risks for the child (e.g. medical, emotional, identity risks). Secrecy and fear drain a family; no one benefits.

Also, remember, you are creating an atmosphere of availability. Your adoptee will make choices, too, as (s)he grows. Not all adoptees may choose to have contact with their birthfamilies. You are just offering that option, in case they want it.

Facilitators

Those people who facilitate any type of adoption, whether it be doctors, lawyers, nurses, social workers, friends, family members or concerned citizens have an important and valuable position. Often the birth and adoptive family members will depend on this outside expertise to guide them through unknown territory. It is important that facilitators know the law, as well as the emotional and the social aspects of adoption. It is important they are aware of all the alternatives available to families and that they present them to each client fairly and without bias.

To choose a knowledgeable facilitator is one of the primary steps in proceeding in any type of adoption. Some families do everything themselves, but usually there are a number of people directly involved in the process. If you find as you interview facilitators that you know more than they do about certain areas, you will need to evaluate whether you want to spend the time educating them and if they are capable of supporting and enforcing your type of adoption. Trust your own feelings about how to proceed. Remember always that this is your relationship, your family not theirs. No matter how much they know intellectually, they don't have to live with this extended family the rest of their lives. They can cash their check and close the file. You need to keep your priorities clearly in mind.

Following is a check list of information you may want to obtain from facilitators when you are interviewing.

LIST OF QUESTIONS TO ASK FACILITATORS

1. What type of cases have they handled in the past?

2. How many cases have they handled and over what period of time?

3. Have they ever handled a cooperative adoption before?

4. Could they give you referrals to persons they have served so you can talk with them?

5. What do they charge? Are there any hidden charges? Is anyone else paying for anything?

6. What specific service do they provide for that charge?

7. Will they provide a written agreement?

8. Will the money be held in escrow/trust until the adoption is finalized? Or what portion of that money will be held in escrow/trust?

9. Will the money be returned if the adoption is not completed? What portion?

10. Who will be receiving money? What amount and/or percentage to each?

11. What specific legal, medical, technical (not emotional or personal) problems do they see in proceeding as you plan a cooperative adoption?

12. What do they require or expect from you?

13. How will the child's rights be protected?

Things To Consider

As you and your family prepare for adoption, as you educate yourselves to the many options, emotions and legalities, there are a number of areas to consider.

Cooperative adoption could involve older children, surrogates, artificial insemination by donor, children with special needs, intercountry, transracial and other possibilities. If all family members can examine the alternatives they will be better equipped to make informed choices.

Deciding what, who, when or if to become part of an adoption extended family is not a whim. It takes careful thought and consideration. Do not limit your thinking. There are all kinds of children and adults who could benefit from expanded family. Following are some of the possibilities for you to consider.

Siblings

Sometimes there are several children from the same family who will benefit by adoption. This could include twins, triplets, full and half siblings. Careful consideration should be given before separating siblings. If it is not possible to raise children together it IS possible to keep them connected through cooperative adoption. Siblings raised in separate households can visit, spend holidays together and continue their relationships. Infants separated will have no say, but toddlers and older children should be consulted and included in the decision making process. This can be difficult because they may have great difficulty understanding why they must live apart. Children can be encouraged to express their feelings rather than to sublimate them.

Fertilization Adoptions

Fertilization adoptions are those that involve artificial insemination, surrogate mothers, embryo transplant and in-vitro fertilization. All utilize a donated sperm and/or egg to create a new life. In each there is either a formal or informal transfer of parental custody by virtue of the fact that the resulting child will be raised by at least one parent to whom (s)he is not genetically related.

There has been an attempt to pretend that these are not adoptions. The inability of our society to accept infertility permeates how these are socially accepted. Now think for a moment about how much secrecy is involved in any aspect of the above methods of creation. IF there is any attempt to hide the genetic connections there is a problem inherent in the process for it does not acknowledge the inalienable right of the child to know his/her genetic heritage, history, roots and relationships.

The methods of documenting and arranging extended family relationships outlined in this book pertain as much to these types of adoptions as to conventional adoptions. There are, however, several preliminary aspects to consider.

1. How will you locate a donor or raising parent?
2. How will you interview them?
3. Who will be included in your decisions and relationships?
4. How will those people respond to a child produced in this manner?
5. How will you, your spouse and family respond?
6. How will you find a doctor/lawyer familiar with handling this type of adoption?
7. How will you continue the relationships you develop?
8. How will the child be progressively included?

If you have discomfort about telling this child the truth, if you won't be thrilled to share this new way of extending your family, thrilled enough to talk freely about it and secure enough to survive others judgement...If you are trying to utilize this method of procreation to hide infertility or genetic connection, then it is not based in human respect and understanding but rather in fear and selfishness. The child is still primary. Not your needs for a child. Parenting in any fashion is serious business whether it is as a sperm donor parent, a surrogate parent, an egg donor parent, a birth, adoptive, foster, custodial or non-custodial parent, or any other type of parent our scientific community may invent.

Take your parenting seriously. Not just the day to day parts of it but also acknowledging the full impact of the participation of ALL other family members. Keep the resulting child as the primary focus. (S)he should grow up feeling good, safe, secure and proud to be alive with full knowledge of the truth of his/her life.

Fertilization adoptions can be handled much like any other cooperative adoption. The difference is only in the initial steps.

1. Locate attorneys, doctors and clinics who will facilitate the location of donors or surrogates and the impregnation process. Check in local telephone books. Sometimes hospitals and adoption agencies will be able to make referrals.

2. Interview the facilitators with the same criteria as in **Chapter VII.**

3. Interview donor/surrogate candidates personally. Don't believe that they ALL want to be anonymous. Require a personal meeting so you *know* you are comfortable with the resulting child's family connections.

Older Children

The older a child is and the more aware (s)he is of environment, the more difficult it is to move that child into a new family setting. Children have a great understanding of what is going on long before they are able to verbalize their concerns and questions. Children who have already bonded to a parent figure can be very healthy and can rebond to the next family, but only if the move is done with exquisite care and expertise. Children who have never bonded can create some life-long problems for their families.

If you really want a very young child, particularly an infant, do not adopt an older child simply because that child is immediately available. This is a very different type of placement. There is a big difference between adopting a baby and adopting even a one-year old child. Children go through stages of stranger anxiety somewhere between six and nine months of age and this is a particularly difficult time to move a child. You would need to work closely with somebody who understands child development and separation/loss issues. This would minimize the trauma for the child. If a child must be moved from the birth family into an adoptive family at an older age, the move should be made slowly and with a great deal of explanation. Get to know the other family. Visit back and forth between each other's homes and spend time together. This will help the child feel safe. Have the birthfamily explain to the child the reasons for the move and give the child permission to love the new family. Convey to the child that this is not their "fault". As much as possible, let the child participate in the decision and moving processes. Let the child bring along everything that is important to him/her and certainly put together scrapbooks that include pictures of the child's life. Don't throw away any of the child's belongings even if you think they are old, raggedy or dirty. That belonging could be more important than anything new and shiny. Do NOT change the child's name because that is the a big part of the child's identity. The last name could be changed IF the child wishes. Otherwise both surnames might be appropriate, as in Hamilton-Paxton. Make sure that both you and the child understand why the child is being placed in a new home.

Afford the opportunity for therapy for the older child who may have signs of depression. If the child has been abused and this is one of the reasons the child is being placed, be aware of the special feelings that this child may have. These children may seek to set up abuse in the new home as well. If the child is in school, meet the teachers of the school and find out everything you can about the child's friendships and peer relationships. Get all the medical background you can on the child and talk to the child's doctor. Even if for some reason the child cannot continue to have a relationship with the birthparents because of abuse or other aspects of the child's background, there are often other relatives, foster parents, social workers, or other people in the neighborhood who have played very loving and supportive roles. These people should be invited to continue participation in the child's life. You can create a cooperative adoption even in the most difficult situations. It is a very rare case that would require the child to be totally cut off from his/her past relationships.

Intercountry

It is important to remember that a child coming from another country can have a cooperative adoption. It is most helpful if the prospective adopting family can go to the country of origin, try to understand the country's ways, not just by studying books and hearing tapes but actually visiting there and talking to the people. It is important for the adopting family to see where the child has been living, meet members of the birthfamily whenever possible, and meet those people who have been the child's caretakers. For the child's birth and adopting families to have pictures and recordings can be helpful. The adopting family can record the sounds of the environment, take movies or photos, bring back artifacts of the culture, taste the foods, hear the language, and find people who can keep in touch over the years. The changes that may take place in that country or the home(s) of the child, can be important information and help the child feel a sense of continuity. If families, friends or acquaintances can continue communicating as the child matures it creates an avenue for the child to revisit with a sense of security.

There are intercountry adoptions where birthparents have chosen to send their children to the United States for specific reasons (e.g. poverty, education). In those instances, the families in the United States can keep in touch directly with the birthfamilies. There are other intercountry adoptions that involve orphans or abandoned children and in these cases the caretakers become important. It is wise to request ALL background information on a child from another country. More often than not there is a great deal of information on the birthfamily, but the orphanages and agencies are not accustomed to facilitating cooperative adoptions. It may take some educating, but many will respond supportively.

Transracial/Transcultural

It is very important to think ahead before becoming involved in a transracial or transcultural adoption. If you are planning a cooperative adoption, know that you will become part of another culture in a very active way. Just as there are signs of readiness to adopt, there are also signs of readiness to consider when adopting transracially or transculturally. Self-esteem and racial identity develop as two separate entities. Both are needed to develop a whole identity. Cooperative adoptions are most important in this form of placement because it allows the child to maintain his or her racial identity. If you want your child to feel comfortable living in both the minority and majority cultures, it will be helpful for the child to have active role models from his/her own racial background, people who are actually friends of the family, or relatives. The adopting family must consider themselves a mixed racial or transracial family. Bicultural socialization must be provided for the healthy identity development of the child. A black or hispanic child moving into a white family does not become white. Instead the family becomes mixed racial. This can affect where the family works, prays and lives.

It is a good idea to carefully examine the whole families racial attitudes. What kinds of jokes are told about other people or other races? Can you have an open discussion with all members of the extended families present? Do you have friends of other races and religions with whom you regularly socialize? This is not something that you suddenly decide to do. It must be a part of your lifestyle.

Adopting families should ask themselves if they are ready to be active anti-racists? Do they have the kind of assertiveness to march or picket in support of their children?

Remember that this is an intergenerational issue. Not only is the child of a different racial background but so will their children and grandchildren be of that background. Will the extended family accept the transracial/transcultural relatives? How do they feel about interracial marriage? Extra sensitivity and understanding of racism are necessary as we live in a race-conscious society.

By having a cooperative transracial/transcultural adoption the child will have many needs met because (s)he is not severed from birth relatives. Support organizations and other transracial/cultural families can be helpful.

Children Born With Handicaps

A cooperative adoption plan should always include discussion (before the child's birth if possible) about what the families will do if the child is born with some type of medical or intellectual impairment. This is a difficult thing to discuss because no one really knows how they will react nor do they want a negative perspective. If the prospective adopting parents only want to proceed in the placement if the child is healthy, the birthparent(s) must be informed so they can base their decisions clearly on this eventuality. Contingency plans should be discussed with the attorneys, doctors, and perhaps local adoption agencies. This will be particularly important in cases where the birthparents know there may be high risk possibilities to the birth of their child. The birthparents may want to carefully consider the kind of adopting family who would be equipped to nurture a handicapped child. Prospective adopting parents can talk to other families who have dealt with children with handicaps to see if that is within their purveyance. They should consider the insurance and financial stress. There will be extra time requirements as the child may have therapy, doctors appointments and hospital stays. The school systems in the adoptive families area should be checked to make sure that a proper education is available for a child with limitations. There are many things to think about and consider if a child is born with a handicap, for all members of the prospective birth and adoptive families.

Adopting Children With Handicaps

Children with handicaps whose birth families are unable to care for them may be available for adoption. The prospective adoptive family must consider their decision and capabilities carefully because it takes extra commitment, time and vision to raise a challenged child.

Specific understanding of the child's limitations, medical care required, financial aspects and birthfamilies willingness to continue involvement will help family members make informed choices. The handicapped child, too, deserves to be viewed as a progressive participant in the decisions that affect his/her life and relationships. The child should never be ignored or discussed as if not present. Cooperative adoptions offer very special opportunities for a handicapped child by expanding their family support systems.

Financial Issues

Birthparents should check into the types of financial back-up available in their state. Placing a child with other parents only because there does not seem to be any comfortable way to locate financial assistance, is unfortunate. Every state has some type of assistance for housing, medical care and other ongoing needs after the birth of a child. Also, in case there are complications at birth, both prospective birth and adopting parents should know what is available in state aid in case they cannot afford the medical costs.

Financial issues are often a primary consideration for birth and adopting families. Many young mothers are not able to envision how they can take care of themselves, let alone their child. Many prospective adopters envision that the costs would be prohibitive. Of course, having and raising children is expensive.

Financial considerations should not be the only determining factor for either birth or adoptive families. There are ways to raise a child with love and adequate care even with extreme financial hardship. Don't let anyone tell you it is impossible. All things are possible.

On the other hand, it would be remiss to ignore the financial aspects of raising a child. The basics of food, housing and clothing must be provided. Sometimes the family can support the child entirely on its' own. Other times welfare, state aid, church assistance or help from friends is required. There should be no shame in requesting assistance in parenting. The tools for parenting do include adequate finances, and each parent should evaluate the financial situation in conjunction with the emotional, psychological, spiritual and physical aspects.

Illness/Death

Any party, including the child, in an adoption could suddenly become ill. Think through the ramifications of disease and illness. These not only cause financial strain but deplete emotional and physical energy. A mother or father could become incapable, even temporarily, of caring for a child. A child could become something other than the joyful experience envisioned. What plans can you make in conjunction with the other family in case something like this occurs? Would the birthfamily be able to take custody of the child again? Who would become legal guardian if the adopting parents became unable to parent? Whatever decisions are made, they should be put in writing so that others are bound to carry out those decisions.

SECTION II

DOING

How To Find The Child/Parent

The focus of this chapter is to assist you in exploring your options in a cooperative adoption.

1

First, go to a local telephone book and look under ''adoption''. Most yellow pages will list adoption agencies in your area. Call all of the agencies and find out if they are doing cooperative adoptions and if so, how they define them. Make sure that this meets your needs. Keep in mind that cooperative adoption means THE CHILD'S ACCESS TO BOTH FAMILIES and anything less than that is not really cooperative.

Adoption agencies and facilitators can give good support and generally do not charge the birthparents any fees. The fees incurred by adoptive parents are also usually less than those paid when adopting independently. On the negative side, there can also be red tape to deal with and a longer wait involved for the process to be completed. Some agencies do not offer cooperative adoptions.

2

Second, check the laws of your state regarding independent adoptions. If they are allowed, you may next want to investigate the possibillity of an independent placement through the use of an attorney. Some attorneys advertise in the telephone book or in the classified section of newspapers in many towns. You can also call your local bar association and request family law practitioners who have experience in adoptions. The best referrals usually come from friends or acquaintances. Interview the attorneys and see what type of openness they practice in their placements. Again, make sure that your needs are met.

3

Third, after you have gathered all the pertinent information on agency and independent adoptions in your state, you must make a decision as to what direction you wish to take. If you choose to place or adopt through an agency, their process will take over at this point. They will then guide you through the adoption.

If you choose to adopt independently, there are more steps that you can begin to take on behalf of a cooperative adoption placement. Some prospective parents choose to proceed with more than one option simultaneously. You will be anxious, but try to remember that there is value in the process, as it gives you time to sort things out. While you are proceeding with the technical steps you can enhance your decision-making tools by associating with a support group, read/listen/talk to educate yourself, fantasize about the child, and use this as a healthy, pregnant time.

If you decide to pursue an independent adoption, you will quickly learn there is no privacy in this process. The best method of realizing your goal is to let the whole world know that you are looking to adopt. You will need to be assertive; you will have to give up any learned helplessness from days of infertility or immaturity.

Research the advertising laws with regard to adoption in your state. Find out if your state is a member of the interstate compact (which is an agreement between many states protecting the welfare of the child when the placement crosses state lines). Find out about homestudies, who does them and when. A homestudy could mean that before the child is moved from one state to another a preliminary review must be completed by licensed professionals.

4

Fourth, one of the first things you will want to do, after you have chosen an attorney, is to write a one-page autobiographical sketch or resume that can be used to tell people about yourself and your desires related to adoption. It should be typed, on personal stationery, and preferably with your own letterhead. Do not make it longer than one page. Do not lie. You can never tell why an adoptive or birthparent might choose you so it is important to just be honest. You can be general in terms of information about yourself. For instance, you can say college-educated and not have to list degrees or where you attended. You can say you enjoy outdoor sports without going into details of which ones or how often. Include why you want to adopt or relinquish, why this is a good time to adopt, why this is a bad time to parent. Go back and look at some of the signs of readiness and share some of your readiness feelings with the other parents. Your desire and readiness should come through in the letter. Share as much of your personality as you can. Share your desire to have a cooperative adoption and why. Close the letter with the name that you wish to be called and a contact number and address. If you choose to use your home phone number and address be sure you have a recorder or answering service for when you are not available. (Indicate if you will take collect phone calls). Include pictures of yourself, family members, etc. Sample resumes are at the end of this chapter.

5

Fifth, you may also want to develop cover letters which can be sent out with this resume. Perhaps you will want a letter that can be addressed to various physicians and churches asking for their help. You might want personal references from doctors, friends, ministers, attorneys. Ask each of these people to pass your letter on to others. Suggest to people who may send your resume on, that they include an additional personal note when they forward your letter to their contact. This method can be extremely helpful as the receiver will take the request more seriously.

6

Sixth, now that you have this photocopied resume and a photograph, what do you do with them? Look at ways to distribute your information, and remember to keep within the laws of your state. The most logical place to begin is your own address book or Christmas list. Send your resume, photo and cover letter to every friend and acquaintance. Do not be shy. Also, send to doctors, dentists and other professionals you know will support your desire to adopt/relinquish. Carry your resume and cover letter wherever you go so you can give them to people at the beauty shop, school, library, even the grocery store —-in case you encounter a situation that seems appropriate. Remember, you have to be assertive. Think about organizations or institutions to which you belong. Have you, or any member of your family belonged to a sorority or fraternity where you could send your letter? Ask friends and relatives to carry resumes for you. Let your religious leaders know of your intent and ask them to disseminate that information throughout your church or temple. Inform neighbors that you are looking for a cooperative adoption. Also tell your employers.

Check ads in the newspaper to see what is going on in adoption and don't hesitate to pick up the telephone and call when someone has information about adoption in an article or the classified section. Be careful about placing ads of any kind — find out if this is legal in your state.

In the process of sending out your resume to friends and relatives across the country, ask them to also check the laws of their states to see what is legal there in terms of advertising and dissemination of information.

You may also do a mass mailing to obstetricians and gynecologists anywhere in the country; mass mailings should be directed to any group that is seeing infertile or pregnant women. Just make sure that it is legal.

If you are adopting independently and are using an attorney who is familiar with adoption, ask the attorney to let other professionals know of your wishes. Don't forget that nurses and hospitals have contact with both prospective birth and adoptive parents.

Baby brokers do exist in this country and will sometimes advertise their services in different locales. They charge money to find a child and they claim to have contacts all over the world. Be careful, for many of them do not understand or advocate cooperative adoptions. Some of these people walk a fine line bordering on grey/black market adoptions and some are insensitive to the personal and emotional issues of the parties involved.

In summary, investigate all the legal options in your state, both agency and private. Become familiar with the laws governing adoptions in your state and any other state/country with which you may deal. If you are going to find your own placement, you will have to give up a sense of privacy and you will have to be assertive. Good luck on your search for a loving, cooperative adoption.

CHECKLIST FOR FINDING CHILD/PARENTS

1. INVESTIGATE AGENCIES IN YOUR LOCALE - Do they facilitate cooperative adoptions? ☐

2. CHECK LAWS OF STATE(S) PERTAINING TO ADOPTIONS. Are independent/private adoptions legal? ☐

3. OUTLINE ALTERNATIVES FOR FACILITATING INDEPENDENT ADOPTIONS IN YOUR STATE. Can the birthmother travel and live in your state until the child is born? ☐

4. CALL ATTORNEYS AND INTERVIEW THEM. Are you comfortable/happy with the one you chose? ☐

5. DECIDE YOUR DIRECTION IN ADOPTION. Are you going to pursue independent or agency? ☐

6. REVIEW LAWS AND POLICIES ON ADVERSTISING TO PLACE OR ADOPT IN YOUR STATE OR OTHER STATES OF INTEREST. Is it legal to place a newspaper ad? ☐

7. WRITE RESUME, COVER LETTER, AND TAKE PHOTOGRAPHS. Do they honestly represent you and your intent? ☐

8. DUPLICATE AND MAIL RESUME, COVER LETTER AND PHOTO. TO: ☐

    a. Address Books/Christmas Lists.
    b. Doctors/Hospitals.
    c. Lawyers, dentists and other professionals.
    d. Religious affiliations.
    e. Work associates.
    f. Organizations - Sororities, Fraternities, Amway, Mary Kay Cosmetics, Elks, Eastern Star, etc.

9. THINK POSITIVE. ☐

10. HAVE PATIENCE. ☐

11. FOLLOW UP ON ALL CONTACTS/LEADS. ☐

SAMPLE RESUME FOR PROSPECTIVE ADOPTIVE PARENTS

PHOTO

Dear

Twelve years ago when we were married, we had dreams of having a large family. After years of gynecological problems, it became necessary, much to our heartache, for Geraldine to have surgery for a partial hysterectomy.

We are very anxious to adopt a baby, and have explored all the channels available. There is currently a five year waiting list with county and private adoption agencies. We are eager to adopt as soon as possible while we are still young. We are writing to ask for your assistance.

We live in a spacious two story home in a neighborhood with other young families. George attended the University of Michigan and has a degree in Business Administration. During the past fifteen years George has worked with a large Business Products Firm and holds a management position. Geraldine studies nursing at Holy Oak College in Walnut. She enjoys gardening, playing the piano and volunteer work at church. Together we have volunteered our time to the Girl Scouts and Little League organizations in our neighborhood.

We are longing to open our hearts and our home to the baby we so desparately desire. Private, cooperative adoption is an especially attractive alternative for the man and woman who want to choose the adopting family themselves, to place the child immediately, to avoid unnecessary delays and misunderstandings and to continue interaction with the adopting family. It is legal and proper to pay all the mothers maternity-connected medical or hospital and necessary living expenses preceding and during the confinement, and to pay for any travel expense incident to the adoption process.

In anticipation, we have prepared a beautiful nursery in our home. We are anxiously waiting to welcome a new baby and family into our lives. If you should know of a woman/man who wish to place their baby with a secure and loving couple with financial stability, as well as, educational opportunities, please feel free to call us collect day or night at (818) 555-0220, or if you wish you may contact our attorney, Frederick H. Marrs, collect at (818) 555-7770.

Sincerely,

Name
Address
City, State, Zip

SAMPLE RESUME FOR PROSPECTIVE BIRTHPARENTS

PHOTO

Dear ;

Several months ago I became pregnant (we found Susan was pregnant) and realized that we had to examine our lives carefully. After much thought and anxiety I (we) have decided that it is in my (our) child's best interest to place him/her in a permanent adoptive home.

I (we) anxiously await a couple (single parent) who could give our child a stable and nurturing home. I (we) want an open, cooperative adoption. I (we) want to meet with and discuss our child's future with the potential family.

Presently, I am working as a mechanic and Susan is enrolled in City College in Midlands. My (our) family is (is not) supportive of our decision.

I (we) long to make a plan for our child as soon as possible. Cooperative adoption is our only choice so that we feel secure about the family and can maintain an open exchange in the future. It seems the best alternative for guaranteeing continuity and extended support for our child.

It is legal and proper for the adopting parents to pay all the mothers maternity-connected medical or hospital and necessary living expenses preceding and during confinement, and to pay for any travel expenses incident to the adoption process.

If you should know of a couple who can offer my (our) child a safe, secure, loving, nurturing home with financial stability and educational opportunities please feel free to call day or night at (502) 555-2342.

Sincerely,

Name
Address
City, State, Zip

Contact & Meeting

For all parties involved in a cooperative adoption, the first contact can be the most frightening, because no one really knows what to do or what to expect. Each party has hopes and anticipations. Each worries that (s)he will be disappointed or be met with disapproval.

First contact should not be a time to do detailed interviews. It is a time just to say ''hello'', get acquainted, and get a feel for each other. Don't be in a hurry. This is not the time to make a mistake and rush into a relationship. This relationship is forever. The first contact begins a time for evaluation and self-examination, so that the decisions feel good and as comfortable as possible.

What Do We Call Each Other?

The first order of business is what you want the others to call you and what you really want to call them. Mr., Mrs., Miss, Ms., Sir, etc. are all formal and distancing. First names are familiar, acknowledging and can draw people together. There are nicknames and personal preferences that can be communicated as relationships develop. It is important to decide your own self-referencing term and to communicate that to the other parties so you will not harbor tensions. If you prefer ''birthparent'' to ''bioparent'' or ''adoptive parent'' to ''psychoparent'', it is important to say so. What the child will be calling each of you will become important too. Be aware that when the time comes for the child to be using names it is not unusual for him/her to use the same term for more than one person with slight variations. ''Gramma'' or ''Grams'' can be used by a child for two different people, and neither one indicates more or less endearment than the other. ''Mom'', ''Mommy'' and ''Ma'' are all possibilites for the same person or three different people. ''Mother Helen'' and ''Mother Kathy'' or ''Mother Smith'' and ''Mother Jones'' are all ways to indicate relationship and yet differentiate the individuals. Don't get into competition over titles. Be respectful of what others feel.

When, Where, Why?

The first contact between the prospective birthparent/birthfamily and adopting parent/family can be done by telephone, by letter, in person or through an intermediary. Each has its plusses and minuses. Only you and the other parties directly involved in YOUR adoption should make the decisions about first contact, — and all subsequent contact. Do not let attorneys, social workers, doctors or well-meaning friends or relatives influence your decisions. Trust your heart.

THINGS TO CONSIDER

1. Place yourself in the others peoples' positions as best you can. Try to think and feel from their perspectives.

2. How do you feel about the contact? What do you want from the contact? Of what are you most afraid? Are you feeling protective of anyone else?

3. Take a good look at all the information you have about the persons you are about to contact. Do you know anything about their feelings, fears, or emotional makeup? Are you sure that information is correct and not shaded by opinion or conjecture? In what kind of environment do they function? Is it conservative, midwestern, restrictive, small town, religious? Is it city, liberal, alternative? Are they married? Do they have other children? Are their friends and family involved in this decision?

4. Look carefully at the situation in which each of you will be. Will there be a comfortable environment? Is it someone's home territory or new to everyone? Is it neutral? Will they be alone? Will there be a support system either there or close by for each participant? Will family, friends, business acquaintances or strangers be eavesdropping? Will each of you feel the surroundings safe?

Sometimes we must choose to make contact in less than ideal surroundings and circumstances, but if you have a choice take all these things into consideration. Remember that it is usual for all parties to be scared. Trust your intuitions and look out for yourself, as well as all others.

How?

TELEPHONE: If you decide to make initial contact by telephone make sure you have done enough preliminary research to determine the situation and whether a phone call is appropriate.

1. Identify yourself by name. A name eliminates one of the first questions entering the parties' minds. IF they would not yet have any way of knowing your name (by previous conversations with attorney, doctor, friends, etc.) don't worry about it yet. You can explain in a moment.

2. State from where you are calling. Just the city or state is enough.

3. Explain briefly how you got their number, name, etc. Make sure to mention the full name of the party who referred you to them. Remember, they may not have been anticipating the phone call and you want to put them at ease.

4. ASK IF THEY ARE ABLE TO TALK. If they indicate it is an uncomfortable time, ask when it would be most convenient and make a definite arrangement for when you will call back or when they may call you. If they are able to talk ... it's now or never!

5. Make sure you leave your name, address, phone number and any other information important for them to be able to reach you.

6. Make arrangements for future contact.

LETTER: Writing can vary from non-commital form letters to specific introductions. It is necessary to make sure your name, address, phone number and purpose for the letter are included. It is also wise to include who referred you and some personal background. If this letter is to be an introduction, you might want to include a photo and other background information.

IN PERSON: The most direct way to have the first contact is in person. Though the first moments can be frightening, this method bypasses many phases of anxiety and fear. Once you have met, there are many areas you no longer can fantasize about! It is important that you give each other a written letter or note containing your name, address, phone number and any other information you wish, so that direct contact can be made in the future.

INTERMEDIARY: Often, by the time of initial direct contact between prospective adopting and birth families, an intermediary has done some preliminary communicating for all of you. This may have been a professional, a family member or a friend. Though intermediaries are well-meaning and can be valuable assets, it is important to have meetings between only the primary parties, so they can establish direct relationships. If you are utilizing an intermediary for the first meeting or contact make sure (s)he has been directed thoroughly in your expectations. Make sure (s)he is someone you trust.

Rejection/Acceptance

Treat the other parties as you would want to be treated. Most people are loving, caring beings and given the chance, will handle their own lives to the best of their ability. Pay real attention to what their actions say, not just their words or what others say about them. If you think about it, no one can or does reject someone else. What they reject is something (usually feelings) that they cannot handle within themselves. YOU cannot be rejected by anyone but yourself.

Promises

Don't make promises you can't keep. Most of us are so anxious to be accepted that we put on our best front and hope that no one will see the real us. Know that what is good in you, about you, and for you is good for all of humanity. Promises made under duress of acceptance or rejection often end up being broken or resented. Promises set up limitations and though those limitations often feel okay at the time, they can not bend and grow with the persons involved. It is best to promise only that you will always try your best to consider that each of you has feelings and needs, and that you will try to be open to the constant renegotiation of relationships.

Time

Believe it or not, you can cherish those first moments of contact when they are in retrospect. So act and react in them as you want to have them in your memory. If you are honest, vulnerable and loving you can feel secure that the outcome of the meeting will be for the highest good of all concerned.

Primary Meeting

Given that the initial contact was successful and everyone felt that (s)he wanted to know more about each other, it is time to set up an in-person meeting. This primary meeting should have simple goals - Getting to know each other better, finding out if you like each other as people, gathering basic background information about each other, and sharing feelings about raising this child.

At this first meeting it would be best to not bring along other children or relatives, and to exclude intermediaries. Take some time for yourselves, where no one has to worry about others. Try to pick an environment where all can be comfortable. Give yourselves plenty of time together and try to leave it open-ended so that you don't have to rush. Give yourselves time following the meeting to process what has happened.

Don't assume anything. Do follow your feelings. Don't be afraid to ask questions. Do be honest and straightforward. You will probably be emotional and that's okay.

PRIMARY MEETING LIST OF QUESTIONS FOR PROSPECTIVE ADOPTIVE PARENTS

1. Why are the birthparents choosing to make a plan for adoption of their child?

2. For what kind of family are the birthparents looking?

3. What is the nature of the relationship between the birthmother and birthfather? Does the birthfather know of the pregnancy and possible adoption plans? How does he feel?

4. Do the extended birthfamily members know of the child? Do they know of the meeting and possible plans for adoption?

5. Why isn't it appropriate for anyone in the extended birthfamily to raise this child?

6. What are the hopes of the birthparents for the child's upbringing? For instance, what are their concerns with respect to religion, education, economic status, extended family involvement, and general lifestyles?

7. What are the expectations of the birthparents regarding the adoptive parents' involvement with them during pregnancy, placement and following finalization?

8. What kind of economic or living needs do the birthparents have during the course of the pregnancy?

9. What has the nature of this pregnancy been for the birthmother? When did she discover she was pregnant? Has she been receiving regular medical care? Have there been any problems with the pregnancy? How has she felt about the pregnancy?

10. Are there any important medical facts to be shared up front with the adoptive family?

11. Do the birthparents want counseling and/or do they have access to neutral parties with whom to discuss their decisions?

12. Would either birthparent accept assistance or support from anyone in keeping, raising and nurturing the child if it became apparent this would be in the best interests of the birthparent and/or the child?

FOR PROSPECTIVE BIRTHPARENTS

1. Why are the adoptive parents choosing to adopt?

2. For what kind of child are they looking and why? (Age, sex, racial background, temperament, physical characteristics).

3. How long have they been married and what is the nature of their relationship?

4. What kind of extended family structure do the adoptive parents have and do those family members know of their plan to adopt? Do they know of this meeting? How do they feel about it?

5. If adoptive parent(s) are infertile how have they coped with that issue?

6. What is the religious background and practice of the family? What are their educational backgrounds?

7. Do the adoptive parents have other children? Are they adopted? What are their names, ages, backgrounds, and hobbies? Are there any medical or emotional problems? Are they gifted or do they have learning disabilities?

8. What expectations do the prospective adoptive parents have of your involvement with them during placement and finalization?

9. What is the adoptive parents' economic situation? What are their occupations?

10. Are there any important medical facts to be shared up front with the birthfamily?

11. Do the adoptive parents want counseling and/or do they have access to neutral parties with whom to discuss their decisions?

12. What are the adoptive parents' hopes for the child's future?

13. What are the adoptive parents parenting patterns? (e.g. authoritative, controlling, strong, disciplinarians, permissive, etc.)

BE DIRECT ABOUT AND SENSITIVE TO YOUR OWN NEEDS.

BE DIRECT AND SENSITIVE TO EACH OTHERS' NEEDS.

THINK FROM THE CHILD'S VANTAGE POINT AT ALL TIMES.

DO NOT COMPROMISE AT THIS STAGE!!!

Subsequent Meetings

Although subsequent meetings can take a variety of forms, including social interaction to become better acquainted, there are additional important matters of personal and business concern.

The location of subsequent meetings can change to more personal and comfortable places. It might be time to meet in each other's homes. Additional family members or other important support systems can be added as you get comfortable. If you were not initially on a first name or nickname basis you should move into that phase. It may be time to share written information with one another.

Begin to compromise and negotiate your relationships and concretize your absolutes. Remember that you cannot negotiate for the child, only for what you are guessing the child will feel, think and want. The best negotiation is one that is open for renegotiation as the child becomes able to participate.

SECONDARY LISTS

BIRTHPARENTS REQUEST FROM ADOPTIVE PARENTS

1. Will you continue contact with the birthfamily and how will you do that?

2. Obtain addresses, phone number, etc. of relatives and friends.

3. Request that a signed Waiver of Confidentiality be placed in files as indicated in the documentation chapter.

4. Determine what, when and how the child will be told of the birthfamily if there is not continued visitation.

5. Determine future plans of the adoptive family. (e.g. will they stay in area or move across country?)

6. Personal history:

Adoptive parents' ages
Places of birth
Nationalities
Parental backgrounds
Siblings of parents
Siblings of child
Date of marriage
Place of marriage
Divorces
Other children in home
  Names, ages, dates of birth
  places of birth, natural or adopted

Medical problems/histories
Deaths in family/causes
Diseases
Citizenship
Education
Religion
Physical descriptions
Photos
Financial history
Professions/occupations

ADOPTIVE PARENTS REQUEST FROM BIRTHPARENTS

1. Will contact with adoptive family continue and what determinates and guidelines will be set?

2. Obtain friends' and relatives' names, addresses and phone numbers.

3. Determine if extended birthfamily and friends will be participating in relationship with the child.

4. Determine future plans of the birthparents. (e.g. marriage, education, career goals, family, geographic location).

5. Prenatal influences need to be discussed. (e.g. alcohol/drug use, nutrition, medications, smoking).

6. Personal history:

Birthparents' ages
Places of birth
Dates of birth
Nationalities
Parental backgrounds
Extended families
Siblings
Other children
Marriages/divorces
Medical problems/histories
Deaths in family/causes

Diseases
Citizenship
Education
Religion
Physical descriptions
Photos
Financial history
Professions/occupations
Time in area/previous residences
Own/rent home
Time in area/previous residences

After primary and subsequent meetings have taken place in which many questions and answers have been exchanged, you are ready to set parameters for your future relationship. By this time you should have established a relationship of true give and take, and a respect for one another's feelings. You should be engaged in type of ''dance'' that feels very natural. Remember throughout everything that you cannot decide for the child what relationship (s)he will have with each of you. You can only decide your relationship with each other and outline the relationship you desire with the child. If you have any unasked questions or indecisions NOW is the time to confront them. DO NOT ENTER INTO AN AGREEMENT UNTIL YOU HAVE DISCUSSED EVERYTHING THAT MATTERS TO YOU. Don't be afraid of sounding foolish...What you're concerned about is probably very important!

Setting Parameters

As you set parameters for your agreement and relationship with the other parents, family and child, remember two things. One, you cannot set parameters for the child, only for yourselves. The child must progressively decide for her/himself. Two, you will often find that you will have an arm in one area and a foot in another as you travel down the path of cooperative adoption.

Cooperative adoption is like any other relationship, in that it is continually renegotiable. What all of you agree on today may not feel so agreeable at a later date. Be flexible. Know this is true for all of you. People change. Encourage that growth and change, maintain an accepting attitude and you will survive.

Build acceptance time into your negotiations. It's always advisable to take time to contemplate and reflect before making agreements. On each step of parameter setting you will find self-examination and learning.

Legalities

Check out each state involved and determine the legal confines. As an example, some counties in Ohio requires the child be placed in foster/child care after the birth while the prospective adoptive parents are being reviewed. In one case, a prospective couple in California had an Ohioan birthmother stay in their home state until the birth took place. This way the adopting family took immediate custody of the child.

Some adoption agencies and practitioners encourage birth and adoptive parents who have agreed on a cooperative adoption plan to utilize agency services to guide them through the process. Since some agencies and practitioners are well versed in adoption procedures this can make things easier. Just remember that neither agencies nor practitioners know everything, and they can be limited in their understanding of how to alter or bend procedures. It is advisable to request everything in writing. Don't let anyone tell you what the law allows without guoting the applicable statutes and sections. If professionals refer to state regulations ask for photocopies of the exact directive on which decisions have been based.

There is usually a way to get things done the way you and your cooperating parents want them.

PARAMETERS ARE FLEXIBLE. A parameter is a constant whose value varies with its application. Don't view it as a barrier or boundary, but rather as a guideline.

Short Term Requirements

MONEY: Talk to each other about what each of you needs and what you can afford. Don't go in over your head and don't underestimate. Better to be safe than sorry. Everyone must live decently, eat and get medical care.

TIME: Discuss what time commitments you can make to each other. Birthparents may need some assistance, such as transportation to and from appointments or the grocery store. Adoptive parents may need extra hours to prepare a nursery. Determine what amount of time you each need for this transition and how you can help each other.

EMOTION: Share with each other the emotional fears, worries, fantasies and joys you are having and anticipate having. Make sure that each of you has an emotional support system and decide how you can support each other. Make sure you discuss what you can't handle and what you expect from each other in the feeling department. This, for some, can be the most difficult area to discuss rationally and about which to make decisions.

RELATIONSHIPS WITH OTHERS: The relationships you have with relatives, friends, co-workers and acquaintances take a back seat during this time. Of course, there are crises that must take precedence, but otherwise give the adoption plan and those relationships priority. Don't be manipulated by the needs of relatives, etc. for attention or credibility. Instead, require that they be supportive, peripheral participants and understand your priority needs for this period of time. Especially, don't let them take over!

Coping With Conflicts

Conflicts can be viewed as negative and insurmountable, or as positive and negotiable. There are some simple tools for dealing with conflicts when they arise.

CONFLICTS

1. Ask to whom it is more important and why?
2. Keep in mind that nothing is forever, so you may be able to live with the other parties' needs for a time.
3. Things can be tried. Businesses have "pilot projects" to see how things work and you can do the same. Don't be resistant to trying different alternatives.
4. Never diminish or attack the other party. Instead, remember that they are human beings with inner struggles, too. You can love them even when they are asking more of you than you think possible to give.
5. Take some neutral time. Usually there is a way to take time to reevaluate and regroup. The decision can usually wait.
6. Neutral parties can give unbiased insight and sometimes come up with a creative solution that will be comfortable to all of you.
7. Compromise. No one should ever feel (s)he has "lost". The art of cooperative relationships is for everyone to win.
8. If you are unable to make decisions, take action. Sometimes any action will break the impasse. Get outside help if you are immobilized by conflict.
9. Remember that there will be some things that cannot be decided now. You will have to trust that time may bring some answers.

Do We Have An Agreement

Ah ha! Here is the moment of truth. Has all the effort, time and energy brought you to a place of agreement or a place of impasse? If you all feel you have had your questions answered, your conflicts stabilized and you are comfortable with what you've discussed, you can shake hands (or hug) and move into the finalization stage. Remember, you cannot make your final decisions until the child is born and is a reality to all of you. But you can know whether or not you are comfortable enough to proceed with drawing up your agreements. Do not ever try to coerce or manipulate each other by these agreements, or make the others "keep their word", or "stick to the contract". You cannot make a contract over a human being, you can only make agreements based on intent and good faith. These agreements are continually renegotiable.

There are four primary points in making an agreement:

1. DETERMINE YOUR REASONS FOR CHOOSING EACH OTHER.
2. DETERMINE THE REASONS THIS WOULD BE GOOD FOR THE CHILD.
3. DETERMINE WHAT YOU INTEND TO DO FOR EACH OTHER AND FOR THE CHILD.
4. SET YOUR GUIDELINES FOR RENEGOTIATING.

PLEDGE

I, (full name)______________________________, hereby
pledge as the (relationship)________________________
of the child named (list full adopted name of child)____________
'nee (list full birth name of child)________________________
that to the best of my ability I will:

1. Be Honest
2. Never Withhold Information
3. Provide Financial Support
4. Provide Medical Care
5. Continue Accessibiltiy
6. Provide Educational Opportunity
7. Answer Your Questions
8. Respect Your Genetic Heritage
9. Assist You In Obtaining Information I Do Not Have
10. Respect Your Individuality
11. Maintain Pride In Your Racial, Religious, Cultural Heritage
12. Work At Maintaining My Marriage and Family
13. Work At Maintaining My Physical and Emotional Health
14. Offer Fair Discipline
15. Listen To You
16. Share My Home and Family
17. Establish A Trust/Inheritance
18. Share Parenting Responsibilities
19. Hold, Love and Nurture You During Your Formative Years
20. Teach You What I Know Of Life and Relationships

*Choose from this list or add as you feel fits your situation.
Extended family may wish to participate in a pledge.

Because I care about your life and the genetic and environmental connections that influence it, I acknowledge and support all those connections and the importance of access as you grow to maturity.

Signed______________________________Date:________________

Bowing Out

Any parent can stop at any point. All of you have the right to bow out BEFORE finalization. There may be loss and pain but better to do it now if it isn't 100% right than to regret it later. BOW OUT COOPERATIVELY. Protect each other, not just yourself. You have each invested time, effort, energy and emotions and you really can help each other through this phase too.

If you feel you can't proceed with this relationship: discuss it, be honest, be sure - (don't cry wolf), and act.

Some of the reasons people cannot proceed with a cooperative adoption relationship are:

1. THEY AREN'T READY. Maybe they are too scared, have really discovered this is not what they want, or have found another situation that is more conducive to their needs.

2. THIS IS NOT THE RIGHT RELATIONSHIP. The value systems are conflicting.

3. MISREPRESENTATION. Misinformation was given which destroyed the trust. The other parties misrepresented themselves or the situation.

4. CAN'T NEGOTIATE DIFFERENCES. There may be legal, geographic, religious, or other problems that can't be surmounted.

5. THE PROSPECTIVE ADOPTIVE MOTHER GETS PREGNANT. If the adoptive couple was intending to build or add to their family by adoption, and the prospective adoptive mother gets pregnant, everyone will have to reevaluate, because two new children were not part of the original plan.

6. MEDICAL PROBLEMS. Sickness, disease, accidents can all happen without warning. This includes birth defects or other medical problems that the child may have. Hopefully, the child's possible medical problems will have been considered and all parents will have made prior decisions or an alternative plan. Evaluation is definitely in order, but none of these things are absolute reasons to bow out. Reevaluate and renegotiate quickly, sensitively, sensibly and jointly.

7. MONEY. Too little money can be a problem because it limits the parties, can restrict how they proceed, and often leaves someone's needs unmet. Too much money already invested can be a problem as the parties involved may feel obligated and unable to bow out. Too much or too little should not be used as an excuse to or not to bow out. If nothing can be worked out to alleviate money pressures an agreement may be made that is not in the best interests of all parties.

8. BIRTHPARENT(S) DECIDE TO KEEP CHILD. The birthparents may discover that they really can't separate from their child.

If you find that any party of your cooperative adoption needs to bow out, allow him/her to do so gracefully. Tell the other people yourself. Don't send a telegram or have someone else do it because you are frightened. Make sure you consider practical problems. For example, if the birthparents have signed relinquishments to an agency and the adoptive parents decide to back out, the birthparent(s) may not be able to regain custody. The agency has the authority to choose new parents. Take responsibility for your decision. You have taken a journey together; you are traveling companions. Don't abandon each other. You can grieve together at the loss. You can assist each other in finding a new cooperative adoption that will better fit everyones' needs. You can continue to touch each other as loving human beings. You can be friends the rest of your lives, and even tell the child the story of how that adoption did not come to be.

The Event

Hospital/Doctor/Delivery

Many birth/adoptive families who have worked closely in a cooperative mode during the pregnancy find themselves frustrated at the point of delivery and after by hospital policies or particular personnel. Since the hospital stay can be an emotionally charged time for everyone involved (as are most births), it is important to set the scene as much as possible beforehand.

Usually the birthparent(s) will have a tour of the hospital automatically. The prospective adoptive parents should also tour the hospital if the birth and adoptive parents have agreed that they are to visit or participate in this phase. In addition, speak to the social workers and the doctor and let them know of your plans and desires. Meet head nurses on different shifts. Check out hospital routines regarding adoptions. See if a private room can be arranged for the prospective adopting parents to spend time alone with the adoptee. Will extended family members be allowed to spend time with the child?

This may seem like extra effort but it will be well worth it. Hospitals are still in transition about many progressive practices and rather than be confronted with the problem of staff limiting or refusing the parents desired interaction, it is wise to take care of as much of this as possible beforehand.

Remember that birthparents can make demands, it is their child. The birthparents can let the staff know how they want visiting to occur. The birthparent can decide about time with the baby, naming the baby, whether or not to hold, feed and nurse the baby, and who will leave the hospital with the baby and in what manner.

Adopting parents need to support the birthparents in having special time with the child. It is healthier in the long run for the birthparents to see the baby, talk to the baby and say their special good-byes. Dr. Thomas Verny, author of *The Secret Life of The Unborn Child* suggests that birthparents and adopting parents should verbally explain to the infant what is happening. Even though the child may not understand the words (s)he pick up on the feelings.

The birthparents' extended family and friends should also have the opportunity to see the child. Pictures can help preserve these memories for everyone. The birthfamily may want to send along some special gift. There may be valued religious ceremonies to be considered.

Three processes are taking place in these vital days after birth:

1. Birthparents are starting to separate, to say goodbye, and to begin their grief process because they won't be the custodial parents.

2. Adoptive parents are starting to bond and feel entitled to the child.

3. The baby is adapting to its new world.

All three are very important things. Everyone needs support, time and understanding.

Celebrating

Many birthparents have shared that they would like to see the birth of their child celebrated just like any other child's birth. They would enjoy receiving notes of congratulations, flowers, and special gifts for themselves and their baby. They may not be the custodial parents, but they did bring this child into the world and have made active plans to see how their child will be raised. They believe that this birth is cause for celebration. Instead, they very often feel isolated and, while the adoptive parents are celebrating, they are left only with their grief. Take the time to celebrate.

Fathers

Many adopting fathers have shared that they have more difficulty bonding to their adoptee than did their wives. Because they were not close to the pregnancy, and even felt somewhat awkward being close to this pregnant woman who was not their wife, they frequently felt left out. Many were not a part of the coaching or were not allowed in the delivery room at the time of the birth of their child. They felt the birthmother was awkward with them and didn't ask them questions or include them in the process. They found it more difficult to go along with the idea of cooperative adoption, and couldn't really tell how they were going to feel after the baby came into the world, or if they could bond and feel entitled to fathering this child. Many fathers shared that they would have appreciated not having so much pressure put on them to make decisions. They would also have appreciated more inclusion in the process.

Birthfathers have often been ignored or left out completely. Sometimes this is because of their own fear or choice but often it is because others presume they don't want involvement, or feel their involvement complicates matters. They have a right and a duty to participate in the decisions that will affect their childs' life. They too need to say goodbye, grieve and celebrate. They need most of all to be acknowledged and not negated. Many birthfathers have stated that though they are not ready to be custodial parents, and possess neither the economic nor emotional tools or maturity required for raising a child, they can participate in the celebration of birth, life and planning for the future. Active participation in decision making makes reflection easier. Deciding to become a non-custodial parent is not ducking responsibility. It is being responsible. Birthfathers and adoptive fathers need more active participation in the process.

Extended Family

Extended prospective birth and adoptive families also feel awkward. They need time to get ready to be custodial or non-custodial grandparents, aunts, uncles and siblings. They also need to acknowledge their own grief work about the loss of biological kinship. They need to have their roles defined and to understand what expectations the parents have of them and how society will react. They need to talk about what they want and expect. Most of all, they need some type of opportunity to learn about the cooperative adoption process and what an extended, cooperative adoptive family means.

Adoptive and birth siblings should be included in the education, evaluation and decision making process. Though they may not actually be able to decide whether there will be an adoption or not, they need to feel they have some value in extending their family relationships. Siblings have an investment in their brothers and sisters. They are either going to have to share their day to day life with them, or lose that day to day exchange. Make sure that birthsiblings have the opportunity to say goodbye and to understand if and when they will see their brother or sister again. Make sure that adoptive siblings get to meet the birthparents and can welcome the new child into their home. Siblings can be very territorial. Confusion about what is taking place can raise all kinds of insecurity, loss and anger issues.

Many of the traditional myths about adoption are carried by extended family and their belief is that cooperative adoption will be destructive, and that someone will get hurt. Often the adoptive family feels this won't be their own grandchild, niece, nephew, brother or sister. The birthfamily may feel that the child will no longer be their grandchild, niece, nephew, brother or sister. They may feel they are competing with the other family. They may be angry because they don't have any say about these relationships. Whatever their feelings are, they need to be acknowledged even if not acted upon. Every possible opportunity should be available to insure that these types of feelings will not continually impede willingness to participate with this new extended family.

Going Home

FOR THE ADOPTING FAMILY: You, your family and friends may have waited a long time for this moment. You will be tempted to fill the house with people and show off your new relative(s). Please go slowly. You are strangers to each other. New parents are nervous and get tired easily. New babies need time to adjust and new adoptees need time to grieve the mother/father they left behind and get used to the new voices and faces of their families. Be selfish. Give your family time to bond. Dads need to hold their babies too. Don't pass the baby around. Keep a nice, restful routine. Let people look but not touch for a few weeks. Let family and friends help by cooking meals for you, cleaning, answering the phone and doing other chores that will give you time to rest and be with your child. You will know when your child feels comfortable enough for the big celebration.

People will ask a lot of questions. You don't have to tell everyone everything. In fact, you don't have to tell anyone anything until or if you desire. The questions can be exhausting, and right now it is not as important that others understand as it is to focus on yourself and your new relationship.

FOR BIRTHPARENTS: The birthparents will leave the hospital differently. They have left something behind. When they get home there may not be a crew of well-wishers and family to bring presents, cook or help. Yet the birthmom has just undertaken the physical and emotional process that some other family is celebrating. She may need extra help as she recuperates and confronts the reality of her decision. The post-partum blues, so common after pregnancy, can impact especially hard when you do not have your baby with you.

If the cooperative relationship is one where the birthparents can participate in the celebrations given for the adoptive family, it is important that the birthparents do not get relegated to insignificant roles, or sideline observers. Neither should they be the center of attention and overshadow the new family. The child really is the focus, and that should make things easier for everyone.

If the cooperative relationship does not include (for personal or geographic reasons) immediate continued interaction, the birth parents must be aware that they will be confronted with loss and sadness at times, and joy and gain at others. People may be afraid to ask direct questions about the experience, and you may feel isolated or ignored. Other people may be more inquisitive than you wish. Respond to questions as you feel comfortable. It is only their business if you choose to make it their business. Every birthparent needs a post-partum support system outside the adopting family. Friends or family who will talk about feelings and be there to listen or just share when the mixture of emotions surface. If the birthparent became primarily or exclusively dependent on the friendship of the adopting family during the pregnancy, there is danger that the loss issues will seem overwhelming if the adopting family does not now maintain the same kind of interest or involvement. Assisting each other to separate interaction and emotional dependence after the child's birth may be the most important aspect of ongoing trust and cooperation. Here is the time that gentle, humane caring and understanding needs to be verbally and directly communicated. No one wants to intrude where they are not wanted or welcome. Birthparents question how welcome they are once they have delivered the baby. And adopting parents often feel they need to let the birthparent go off and heal by his/herself.

There is a period of weeks or months that can be hard for both the adoptive and birth families. They may have become very close friends. They will now enter into two different processes that separate them. The birthparents are involved in a stage of grieving where they can feel anger and depression. They will be grieving not only the loss of the child, but may also grieve the loss of the close relationship built with the adopting family. They may grieve for the loss of a certain lifestyle attained during pregnancy.

At the same time, the adopting parents are adjusting to a totally new lifestyle. They are bonding with the child which is a mutually sharing and supportive process. They are full of joy.

The two processes of grieving and bonding often do not blend well. There seems to be a time when the adoptive and birthfamilies wish to stay away from each other. They may be able to keep in touch by mail or phone but may not want to see much of each other. What drew them together initially was a need. Now their needs separate and go in different directions. They will have to find a way to become friends exclusive of mutual need. This is usually the first step in renegotiating their relationship. Many families are not able to make promises until after the baby is born. They each need to see how their grief and bonding realities affect their thought processes and then come back together again. This can be a scary time for both parties. All the plans made before the child is born are based on desires, dreams, vision and hope. Now the child is a reality. Now relationships can be negotiated and decisions made that will feel secure and well based. Remember that cooperative adoption is a constantly renegotiated process.

After Placement

While the adopting parents are bonding and becoming entitled to their child, they may also have a certain amount of sadness for the birthmother/father and perhaps some guilt for taking his/her child. If the adoptive parents have given birth, this feeling of guilt may be stronger because they can really feel the birthparent's loss. Many adoptive parents are concerned because they are not sure where their responsibility to the birthfamily begins and ends.

While the birthparents are separating and grieving they may also feel guilty and sad. It seems that birthparents are supposed to "forget", and be thrilled at the joy the adopting family has. When they don't forget, they feel they have failed. When they don't feel thrilled or overjoyed that their child is going to be raised by other people, they may feel guilty.

These types of conflicting feelings are normal. It can be beneficial to communicate that they are occuring and to reassure each other that all feelings are okay. As much as each participant in a cooperative adoption may need to separate and limit communication at times, they may need that communication intensely other times. Cooperative adoption works best when everyone involved has other support systems and friends. This includes the adoptees as they grow up. Without outside support systems and friends we tend to be afraid to experiment with our emotions, take risks in new relationships, or be honest about our thoughts and feelings. Remember that friends opinions and support can fluctuate. Try not to depend entirely on other people's agreement or endorsement of your situation. Sometimes they may not understand. It is possible to turn to people for support even if they do not agree if you respect each other's right to differ in opinion. Support systems are important but you may find that supportive friends and family may change from time to time.

Most Common Questions

Because open, cooperative adoptions seem new in our society, there is a lot of territory without rules. This can make it more fun because you get to think things up as you go along. We are not going to give you definite "yes" or "no" answers to the following questions, but do want you to think about what you gain and what you lose by making different decisions.

1. *DOES THE BIRTHPARENT LIVE WITH THE ADOPTIVE FAMILY? WHERE COULD (S)HE LIVE?*

   If the birthmother lives out of state and needs to be near the adoptive parents at the time of delivery, different arrangements may need to be made. Living together might mean a very special closeness and an opportunity for mutual bonding to the baby through the last few months of pregnancy. It also could make it more difficult if either party decides they do not want to proceed with the adoption. Some people feel that having the birthparent live with the adoptive parents is a subtle form of coercion.

   Sometimes birthparents can stay with other people who have adopted or with other birthparents who have already been through a cooperative adoption. The birthparent may want to stay in an apartment or maternity home or with members of her family in order to maintain her own privacy and support system.

2. *HOW MUCH DO PROSPECTIVE BIRTH/ADOPTIVE PARENTS PAY?*

   In some states the things which can be paid for are clearly spelled out. This may mean prospective adoptive parents can pay only for medical expenses relative to the pregnancy and the baby after birth. For instance, if the birthmother is not allowed to work for a period of weeks before or following the birth, adopting parents may be allowed to pay for her living expenses.

If adoptive parents offer to pay for a college education, a car or other things, it may look like payment for the baby, which is against the law. Some birthparents choose to pay all their own expenses. Family insurance may cover all medical costs and most states provide a form of financial aid or medical insurance for needy mothers.

3. *WILL THE BIRTHFATHER AND PROSPECTIVE ADOPTIVE PARENTS MEET?*

Children have the right to access to information about both the birthmother and birthfather. Without the birthfather, the child will only have half the information that (s)he needs. If the birthfather is not accessible, has refused involvement, or the birthmother won't reveal or doesn't know his identity, the child deserves knowing as much as can be put together under those restrictions.

4. *HOW ARE THE EXTENDED BIRTH AND ADOPTING FAMILIES INCLUDED?*

It can be very helpful for other children in the birth and adoptive families to meet and even for grandparents, aunts, or uncles who may be a major support system to have that opportunity. When we see people in relation to their relatives we often get a larger focus. Seeing a larger family system gives the birthparent a sense of security about how the child will be raised and the adopting parents more answers to give their child. One of the negatives would be that there will be many more people having input into this placement, which sometimes confuses things.

5. *DO ADOPTIVE PARENTS HELP IN CHILDBIRTH COACHING? ARE THEY PRESENT AT THE BIRTH?*

Everyone must be comfortable with participation. This is a very special way to share the child's life before birth and a special knowledge to be able to share with the adoptee as (s)he grows. Birth is a miracle... The celebration and one's birth story are valuable tools in rooting and connecting.

6. *WHO GOES TO THE HOSPITAL AND WHEN?*

Again, everyone must be comfortable with the decision. Adoptive parents might enjoy being able to talk with the nurses, see the baby and even help care for the baby in those first few days. Working together during those days can make the child's transition smoother, adoptive parents transition into parenting smoother, and birthparents' transition and letting go easier. Emotionally there are advantages and disadvantages. Different families react differently. Sometimes there can be a conflict with entitlement issues, such as who gets to leave the hospital with the baby. State laws may dictate your decisions here. The extended family may wish to send flowers or visit. Strive to make sure that EVERYONE is comfortable. The birth and adopting parents are important and their feelings affect how they interact with the child.

7. *DO ADOPTIVE PARENTS OR EXTENDED FAMILY HELP THE BIRTHPARENT AFTER BIRTH?*

This again, will depend upon the types of arrangements and agreements you have made with regard to your ongoing relationship. It will depend upon the needs of the birthparent and who are really the best people to meet their needs. It is important, however, for you to remember that your focus now needs to be on this new baby and mutual bonding. If you feel divided between the other parents' needs and your own and the baby's, always choose the baby's.

8. *WHAT ABOUT BONDING?*

Babies bond in-utero to their birthmother by heartbeat, body rhythm and sound. Many experts say they even recognize voices before birth. Prospective birth and adopting parents spending time together during pregnancy can begin the bonding process. The baby can bond to both families. Coaching, being present at delivery, and being available immediately after birth continue to facilitate the childs bonding with the adopting parents. The baby's first bond should be during pregnancy. A birthmother who disconnects from her feelings for her child might cause pre-birth bonding detachment. This could make it difficult for the child to bond after birth to either the birth or adopting parents.

9. DO WE HAVE A BABY SHOWER AND WHO WOULD BE INVITED?

Adoptive parents should have the same enjoyment, celebration and support at the coming of an adoptee into their home as when any other child arrives. Baby showers are certainly part of this. Birthfamilies may want to give gifts and/or a shower to send the child to its new home "in style". If it is part of the customs of your family, it would be important not to deny yourself this pleasure. Whether or not the birthfamilies and adoptive families combine their efforts and celebration is entirely up to them. Do what feels best.

10. WHO GIVES THE BABY A NAME?

Someone must! Many people may want to! Birthparents can name the child and have it entered on the original birth certificate. Adoptive parents can name the child and have the name changed at finalization and entered on the amended certificate. Cooperative naming could include a name chosen by each family. Names are gifts and the adoptee would then gain from everyone and lose nothing. Vital statistics statutes do not limit the number of names given to a child. Each of you probably has names that have meaning for you that you would like to give to the child. (See the suggested cooperative birth certificate on page 107). There are many alternative ways to share in the naming of the child.

11. WHO GETS CALLED MOM OR DAD?

Terms of endearment are not in competition. Some kids have lots of grandmas and grandpas. Kids from divorced families often call all their mothers "Mom" and fathers "Dad". If you have preferences, discuss them, but also leave room for the adoptee to choose for him/herself.

12. WHAT IF THE OTHER PARENTS WANT MORE/LESS OPENNESS THAN I DO?

If you are unable to comfortably agree on the degree of openness in your relationship and interaction with the child, it is advisable to withdraw from a commitment to this particular family and wait for one that is more what you want. Don't rush into or hold onto any family as your only choice. Don't let desperation or time pressure you into a decision that is not comfortable for all of you. You will have to live with these relationships and parameters for a long time. Your child will have to live with these relationships too.

13. *WHAT IF THE OTHER PARENT(S) WANT TO BACK OUT AFTER I HAVE MY HEART SET ON THEM?*

It will be disappointing and you will be hurting emotionally, but it is best for everyone to do what feels right to him/her. All relationships are a risk and this is no exception.

14. *WHAT IF THE OTHER PARENTS CHANGE THEIR MINDS AFTER THE ADOPTION IS FINAL?*

Once the adoption is finalized by the court, the legal custody of the child is with the adoptive family. Unless there was fraud involved, there is probably no way the court would return custody to the birthfamily. Of course the adoptive family can choose to relinquish rights and responsibilities just as can any parent. Everyone involved should try his/her best to make sure that concrete decisions have been made so the child does not end up in a custody battle.

15. *HOW DO WE TELL OUR CHILD(REN) ABOUT ADOPTION?*

One of the beauties of cooperative adoption is that you won't ever have to tell as the child will always know. The child will have access to any information which (s)he may need from both families. The child may need help in integrating that information. It will be important as (s)he grows that there is a clear understanding of who is the parent in charge. The cooperative families must keep their information straight. Neither family must lie to the child. If there is some particularly difficult information to share, the families should agree when it should be shared and by whom. If either family has other children, they too must be told the truth. The process and reasons need to be explained to other children to help alleviate any anxieties they may have about being "left" too. Birthsiblings need to be reassured that their brother or sister is alive, safe and well. They need the same opportunity to visit or see pictures. All children need to understand that nothing is their "fault". Family secrets on either side can make families crazy. One cover-up leads to another and before long the family experiences undue and unnecessary stress. Many children in our contemporary society live with parents and family members who did not conceive or birth them. Your children are dealing with step-families, single parent families and divorce, as well as adoption, in their school settings regularly and with their peers. If the adults in a childs life are comfortable, the child will find comfort and security.

These questions must all be answered by the participants in your adoption and they must be answered to everyone's satisfaction to remain in a comfortable, cooperative, working relationship. Remember that when negotiating relationships everyone must win.

Cooperative adoption is a WIN/WIN situation. Nobody loses.

Mediation How-To's

Mediating adoptions can be done by yourself, your family members and/or professionals. No matter how many outsiders you request assist you in establishing these relationships, you will still always have to resort to knowing how to mediate on your own behalf.

Mediating is necessary when there are conflicts. As you establish and renegotiate your relationships you may find that conflicts do arise. These conflicts of needs, desires and opinions will change over the years but each must be dealt with in a positive, mutually endorsing fashion.

There are a number of basic tools. Each person must feel secure in knowing they won't lose. If all of you commit to a WIN-WIN rather than a WIN-LOSE relationship, everyone will feel more secure. Each person must feel competent, and must feel they are viewed as competent. Each person must trust their own integrity and the integrity of the others. If everyone feels they are part of the adoption extended family and that they will continue to be respected in the decision making process, they will feel more secure.

Identify each persons feelings. Give credibility to anything that anyone expresses they feel. Even if you don't understand how they can feel that way or why, trust that they do know how they feel better than you can. Acknowledge how they feel. Don't argue with their feelings, or tell them they shouldn't feel that way.

Listen. Assist each other in clearly identifying what you want. Respond in non-defensive ways. Don't defend your position or anyone else's. Stay focused on the central idea, which is that this relationship matters to you and that the other people matter to you, and you matter to them.

When one of you has a problem communicating, check to see if you are all focused on the relationship or if there are other things distracting you. Determine who owns the problem, what the problem is, what behavior is involved and if any people not present are involved. In adoption when dealing with an infant or young children, mere physical presence does not mean they are able to voice or fully participate on their own behalf. Some criteria for representing them must be established. No one parent or set of parents will ever be a complete representative so therefore it may be best to have an outside, versed mediator represent the child's interests (e.g. another adoptee or close friend of the child) or agree that you will mutually represent the child's interests until the child is able to represent him/herself.

Set a specific time and place and other ground rules with some reflection time if possible. When you come together follow these guides:

1. Define the problem as specifically as possible.
2. Never negate anyone elses definition of the problem as they see it.
3. Brainstorm possible solutions together.
4. Evaluate the solutions proposed.
5. Determine by concensus the solution you would like to try.
6. Determine the amount of trial time.
7. Initiate the solution and practice it as fully as outlined.
8. Come together to review and reevaluate at a predetermined time.

Make plenty of room for your differences. Do not use punishment of any kind to make a point, get even or get your way. Acknowledge that the power in these relationships can change from time to time. In the beginning the fertile parent holds the power. After custody is legally transfered the custodial parent holds the power. In the end the child holds the power. Know that you want to be treated as fairly as you treat others. Everyone takes a turn.

When any party is not handling their own problems or emotions it becomes acceptable to renegotiate and redefine the relationship until they do. This rule gives all parties permission not to ''babysit'' the others problems and remain responsible only for their own participation. Be aware that everything influences a persons life and they may be bringing outside problems into your relationship.

Probably the most difficult part of mediation is keeping in mind that everyone is right. Each person may be as right for themselves as you are for you. You may view others decisions as wrong for you. That is okay. But be careful not to project that those decisions are also wrong for the other person. It always comes back to what is good for the child. There is no easy, wonder drug solution to negotiating relationships, but if everyone keeps the relationship itself as primary, solutions will surface.

Everybody Counts

It follows here to take a moment to reinforce that EVERY MEMBER of an extended family COUNTS. If anyone is claiming to be championing someone else's needs they should stop and reexamine. Chances are they are hiding behind those projected needs. If all participants can talk in the first person saying ''I feel'', ''I need'', ''I want'', they can claim their own feelings, thoughts and desires. Communication will be more direct and productive if all parties claim their own feelings.

Evolving Relationships

How you define your relationships today will not be how they are tomorrow. Each person changes. Every cell in our bodies change every eleven months so how can we presume to stay the same, or hold anyone else to who they were? We can nurture growth, change and development in others, as well as ourselves. We can assist them in feeling endorsed as they struggle with their own progress. The most dangerous thing any of us can do in any relationship is to carve a person, their actions and responses in stone. It chokes the growth and flowering of a relationship.

Gentle evolution is most desirous but not always attainable. Sometimes change is abrasive and uncomfortable. Sometimes birth and adoptive families have different values and lifestyles, and these may be respected or criticized. The best evolution tool is evaluation. This allows each person to observe a situation or behavior, and without being critical or judgemental, decide if it is admissable in their preferred environment.

Relationships change because people change. The more each person can flow and trust and feel secure with change, the easier relating will be.

Changing Closed Adoptions Into Cooperative Ones

The last several decades have reflected a presumption that adoptive and birth families need to be protected from each other. In fact, over half the adoptions that occur involve some communication and exchange by the parties involved. If you are involved in a closed adoption situation and wish to change it into an open one, there are a number of things to consider.

First, do you know where the other parties are or are you going to have to undertake a search in order to locate them? If you do not know where they are, are you willing to take the time, effort and energy to undertake such a search? If you are, you will find quite a number of organizations and search professionals able to assist you. Even if you know the identity of the other parties, you may not know exactly where they live today. Triadoption Library's International Referral Service lists hundreds of groups, consultants and resources of value to a searcher. (See Appendix).

Second, determine your priorities. It is of great value to understand your own motivation. It is okay to be making a decision to open up a closed situation. It does not mean the other parties will want the same openness you do, but you will not know until you speak with them. If your desire is simply to have current information, you have several alternatives. a). Utilize an intermediary or liason to transfer information. b). Request this information in written form. c). Request photographs. d). Make personal contact by phone, letter or mail.

Third, you can decide that you want a relationship with the other people. Remember that they may not want a relationship but that does not preclude you from telling them your wishes.

Maybe most important is that you want acknowledgement from other human beings. This acknowledgement is not only of everyone's existence, but of their value as friends, relatives or acquaintances. You may be requesting that your relationships become renegotiable. You will be taking risks emotionally and asking others to do the same. There should be no reason this cannot work if everyone will be gentle and cooperative. Don't demand things be entirely your way. Don't allow others to negate your needs and wishes entirely either. Each party to an adoption is part of an extended family and will have to determine their participation in each relationship for themselves. And that includes the child as (s)he progresses in cognizance.

Probably the most difficult aspects of changing an adversarial adoption into a cooperative one is the patience it takes. If any party does not wish to cooperate it becomes impossible for the others to have clear relationships. Non-cooperation is manipulative behavior and always requires that one party be given more credence than the others. Cooperative relationships acknowledge that everyone has equal credibility and should therefore have equal negotiating and relating abilities.

A good guideline to determine balance is to ask yourself if you are keeping the childs ability to negotiate in mind. If you determine your needs independent of those of the other parties that is fine, but to cooperate you must all have your needs acknowledged, and there must be a balance established which meets equal amounts of everyone's needs. Whenever anyone's needs are negated, diminished or belittled there is an adversarial situation in the wings.

How do we make the change from adversarial to cooperative? From closed to open?

First of all, closed to open is quite easy. This involves only knowledge of identities. *Cooperative* on the other hand involves not only knowledge of each other's identities, but relationship and interaction. This relationship and interaction may be constant or periodic. The parties may agree not to interact for long periods of time, but the ability to renegotiate that agreement is always respected.

Telling

Explaining the extended family and adoption to others is only difficult if a). there have been lies or secrecy involved, b). the telling party is not comfortable with the truth. Therefore it is important to work through your own discomfort so you do not project this to the child or other family members.

Changing a closed adoption into a cooperative adoption involves accepting that no one needs to be protected from the truth, trusting that people can handle all the information and that you'll be there for them as they assimilate change.

Take a quiet time to reflect on those areas that feel uncomfortable and try to pin point both reasons and answers. Discuss your feelings and anxieties with others who have confronted similar experiences. There are books and tapes available where people share these experiences. (See Appendix).

After you have worked through your own feelings you should choose an appropriate time and setting. This should not be set up as an intense event. Examine your family structure and interaction. Are there times set aside for family discussion? If there seems to be no ideal time you will need to create the next best thing. Waiting until an "opportune" moment can delay the telling too long. The longer you carry the "secret" the more chance the other people have of feeling duped or untrusted.

Sharing your own feelings can make this very real for all parties and possibly help them feel safe and secure with their own feelings. People learn to survive emotional strain by observing others doing it. Remember that this does not have to be an anxious time, it can be a thrilling and joyous time. You are adding information and relationships to you and your families lives.

Include time to discuss each others feelings. If anyone does not want to share, give them time and then bring the subject up again. Adoption is a continuing relationship. It is not something to be discussed once and presumed final. It evolves and the participants feelings evolve and change. "Telling" does not need to be a front page headline or public announcement. It can be intimate sharing.

"Telling" really is the time when all parties are given all available information. At the very least, involved parties are informed that relationships exist and that more information is available on request.

SECTION III

DOCUMENTING

Documenting The Adoption

Documenting an adoption fully is done so that no one can take advantage of any other party. Documentation protects the child's interests and prevents the adults from reneging on the agreement to cooperate, negotiate and maintain some type of communication.

A truly cooperative adoption would not seal the court record nor eliminate any of the birth names from the certificate of birth. It would add the adoptive parents' names and possibly add given and surnames for the child. At this time some judges, courts and states are still insisting on sealing the court record and altering the birth certificate. Make sure that you request that the court does not seal the record or the original certificate of birth, and that the agreement to maintain communication and non-sealing is written into the adoption decree. This will place parties who do not comply in contempt of court and reinforces everyone's commitment to their agreement. Whether the records become sealed or not should not influence the diligence with which all parties acquire the documents and records on themselves and each other.

What follows is a break down of records that should be obtained by both the birth and adoptive families and put away for safe keeping. It is recommended that a complete set be placed in a safety deposit box or other holding in the adoptee's name, as their property, with no restrictions on their access. Banks have different rules in this regard but usually allow an adult as trustee until the child has reached majority.

The best rule to remember as you document your adoption and interact with the system is NEVER ACCEPT *NO* AS AN ANSWER! Almost always there is a way to do and to get what you want if you want it badly enough. Don't place yourself in battle with people or argue with them. Simply resolve that you will take the time and make the effort to find an alternative.

Attorney's Legal Papers

An attorney begins a file as soon as either party meets with him/her and requests services. Explain on this first visit that you must receive copies of ALL records added to your file. It might be a good idea to draw up a written agreement to that effect which includes the right of the adoptee/birthparent/adoptive parent to have viewing or copies upon demand. A suggested format follows:

Attorney/Client Agreement

A

AGREEMENT BETWEEN

ATTORNEY: (attorney's name) ____________________

AND CLIENT: (client's name) ____________________

This is to confirm the client's right to view and obtain photocopies or microfilm copies of all documents and records held in files by this attorney and/or his office.

These will be available within a reasonable time after written or verbal request not to exceed fifteen (15) days.

Photocopy or duplication fees and postage will be paid by:__

In addition, the right to viewing and copying will extend to the following people:*

____

____

____

____

SIGNED (attorney's signature) ____________________ DATED: ____________________

SIGNED (client's signature) ____________________ DATED: ____________________

*Be sure to include the adoptee's birth and adopted names, and all other extended family and primary triad members.

Hospital/Medical Records

Medical records are kept by the doctors, midwifes, hospitals, or clinics who see the prospective adoptive parents during infertility testing, the birthmother during pregnancy, and the child after birth. Included here are sample medical forms to be filled out by both the birth and adopting families for their personal files. In addition, we recommend that you obtain all pertinent medical records of pregnancy, birth and peripheral treatment as they are recorded. Also, included is a sample RELEASE AGREEMENT to be signed by all parties which will be placed in the doctor's, lawyer's, agency's and hospital's files (and your own files too!) to document ongoing access to these records by all involved parties. (Note: there are restrictions that can be added).

Many states have direct access to medical records only by the parties to whom they pertain. The RELEASE AGREEMENT gives your permission for the copies of these records to be given to the adoptee, adoptive and birth family members indicated, whenever they make such a request. Medical records may be more important at some later date than anyone anticipates at the present time. Also, an adoptee may find them valuable and interesting at some point in life. Make sure all releases include the adoptee's access and are notarized.

Medical Records Request

B

Patient Records
Hosptial/Doctor's Name
Address
City, State, Zip

Dear Doctor/Hospital Administrator;

(We) I request the following from your patient files and/or microfilmed records:

Pertaining to: Full medical, delivery and nursery record, statistics of birth, birth certificate, footprints, physical examinations, discharge and payment record for:

NAME: ______________________________

BORN: ______________________________

HOSPITAL: ______________________________

CITY: ____________________ STATE: ________

DATES OF CARE: ______________________________

Thank you in advance for your time and effort extended to filling this request. If there are any duplicating or mailing fees please indicate and I will pay them promptly.

Sincerely,

Name
Address
City, State, Zip

*If for any reason you did not have a HOSPITAL/MEDICAL RECORDS RELEASE AGREEMENT signed you should indicate your relationship to the party whose records are being requested and include a current signed and notarized release agreement. If you are the legal guardian of the child you can request the child's records but may not be able to obtain birthmother's records without a signed release.

Hospital/Medical Records Release Agreement

C

Patient Medical Records
Hospital/Doctor's Name
Address
City, State, Zip

I, ______________________________ hereby state that I waive all rights of confidentiality extended to self that is granted to me under the statutes of the State of ______________________ the hospital of ________________, and/or Doctor ____________

This waiver of confidentiality and right of privacy is extended solely to those persons listed below: *

____

____

____

____

Permission is granted to the holder of this affidavit to furnish a copy of this transcript upon request to those above named persons and to provide full transcript copies of any files or microform records pertaining to myself, ____________________ or my child, (name) ____________________ born (mo/day/year) at (hospital/clinic name) ____________ in (city/state) ____________ This is to be regarded as full consent for release of all files to those specified.

SIGNED: __________________________ NOTARY:

DATED: __________________________

*Be sure to include adoptee and all other extended family as desired.
**Be advised you should have an attorney draw up a waiver or affadavit.

State/Agency Files

Attorneys or social agencies keep files on every case they handle. Most states have adoption units in the welfare/social services departments which maintain a file for adoptions handled within their jurisdiction. These files are often detailed. DO NOT sign any document with them that gives permission to keep files on you of which you cannot obtain copies. The Freedom of Information Act guarantees the right to "challenge, correct and amend" any federal record kept on an individual. In order to challenge, correct or amend, one must be able to view that record. Besides, you want to know what information is being kept on you, as others may view it to make decisions and suggestions that affect your life. A RELEASE FORM is included here to be filed with the lawyers, agencies and state departments who become involved in your adoption. This should guarantee the release at any future date, of copies of ALL records kept by them to any birth or adoptive family member indicated and to the adoptee on request.

State/Agency Files Release Form

AUTHORIZATION TO RELEASE FILE MATERIALS **D**

I, , hereby authorize the release by , to my adopted daughter, , or her attorneys, , of all documents contained in the file of , deceased, regarding the adoption by me and my husband of said daughter, provided that this authorization shall extend only to those documents the originals of which were filed with the Superior Court of the County of , State of , in case number including but not limited to the and the Report of County Department of Adoptions.

DATED: ____________________

Notary Public

Signature ____________________

State/Agency Files Release Agreement

E

State Department of Health
Address
City, State, Zip

RE: Adoption Files of: ______________________________
____
____

To Whom It May Concern: I (we) hereby grant permission that all sources of records pertaining to my(our) self, ______________ and my(our) child ______________________ be released in full transcript to the parties listed below: *

____

____

____

____

I (we) waive our rights to privacy and confidentiality granted to us under the statutes of the State of ______________________ and the policy of (Name of Agency)______________________. This waiver is extended only to those persons listed and no others. All records and files requested by these parties at any time from this day forward shall be provided within a reasonable time not to exceed fifteen (15) days. Duplicating costs and mailing fees will be paid by (Name of Agency or Individuals)______________________

SIGNED:______________________ DATED:______________

NOTARY

*Be sure to include adoptee and all other extended family desiring access.

**Be advised you should have an attorney draw up a waiver or affidavit.

***Restrictions can be added pertaining to dates of accessibility.

Case Files

The social worker's description and accumulation of records are entered in the agency files, sometimes in the state department's files and sometimes in the court's files. Make sure that you request these records BEFORE the adoption is finalized. Although adoption (e.g. sealing the court record and original birth certificate) is not meant to be retroactive, in practice it is. The sealing process wipes out access to all court and vital records prior to the finalization and is often interpreted by agencies, lawyers, and doctors as meaning that the files are no longer accessible to anyone except their staff. The adoptive parents should request a copy of their home study from the social worker prior to going to court. If the social worker is not cooperative, request the court report from the court, preferrably before you are in judge's chambers. Remember, NOTHING IS SEALED UNTIL THE ADOPTION IS FINALIZED. Of course, if the judge agrees to omit sealing the court record and the birth certificate, you have no problems.

Documents

The primary documents in any adoption are described and samples included here. They vary from state to state and sometimes from year to year, but these should give you an idea of what to be looking for.

Medical Consents

Birthparents must sign a medical consent and hospital release for the child to be removed from the hospital by anyone other than themselves. The medical consent gives permission for the adoptive family to obtain medical attention and treatment for the child until there is court acknowledgement of the custody transfer.

Hospital Release

F

State of California—Health and Welfare Agency

HEALTH FACILITY RELEASE REPORT OF MINOR TO OTHER THAN A PARENT OR LEGAL GUARDIAN

Prepare original and 3 copies: one copy each for hospital file, natural parent, and person receiving minor.

Send original to: State Department of Health (Within 48 hours as required by Health & Safety Code Section 1283)
744 P Street
Sacramento, California 95814

IMPORTANT NOTICE

THIS HEALTH FACILITY RELEASE FORM IS NOT A RELINQUISHMENT OR CONSENT FOR ADOPTION

IN CALIFORNIA THERE ARE TWO BASIC WAYS A CHILD MAY BE PLACED FOR ADOPTION IF THE PARENT FEELS THAT SUCH A PLACEMENT IS IN THE BEST INTEREST OF THE CHILD:

1) THE PARENT MAY PLACE THE CHILD DIRECTLY WITH ADOPTIVE PARENTS. THE PARENT RETAINS ALL RIGHTS TO THE CHILD'S CUSTODY AND CONTROL UNTIL A CONSENT TO THE ADOPTION BY THE PETITIONERS IS SIGNED BY THE NATURAL PARENT(S) IN THE PRESENCE OF AN AGENT OF THE DEPARTMENT OF HEALTH OR A LICENSED ADOPTION AGENCY. ONCE GIVEN, THE CONSENT MAY NOT BE WITHDRAWN EXCEPT WITH COURT APPROVAL.

2) THE PARENT MAY RELINQUISH THE CHILD TO A LICENSED ADOPTION AGENCY FOR PLACEMENT IN A HOME APPROVED BY THE AGENCY. ONCE THE CHILD IS RELINQUISHED TO A LICENSED ADOPTION AGENCY THE RELINQUISHMENT MAY NOT BE RESCINDED EXCEPT BY MUTUAL AGREEMENT.

I. IDENTIFYING INFORMATION

Child's Name ____________ Birthdate ________ Sex ☐Male ☐Female

II. PARENT'S AUTHORIZATION (Fill out completely before parent signs. Alterations or deletions invalidate form).

A. I ____________, the parent of ____________
authorize ____________ Hospital to release my
child to ____________ residing at (complete
address) ____________. In releasing my child from
hospital for the purpose of ☐ Adoption Planning, ☐ Foster Care, ☐ Other, Explain
____________, I retain all parental rights to his/her custody
and control. This only authorizes release of my child from the hospital.

B. MEDICAL AUTHORIZATION

I authorize and empower the person(s) named in Section II A above to make any provisions for medical and surgical care for my child identified on this report, including anaesthesia, which may be deemed necessary or advisable by any licensed physician, for a period not to exceed three months from the date of my child's release from this hospital.

________ (Witness) ________ (Date) ________ (Signature of parent, or person having legal custody of child)

III. ACKNOWLEDGEMENT BY PERSON(S) RECEIVING CHILD

I/we have on this date ________ received (child's name) ________
for the purpose of ☐ Adoption Planning, ☐ Foster Care, ☐ Other, (Explain)
____________. I/we understand that this only authorizes release of this child from the hospital. This is not a consent or relinquishment of this child for adoption.

________ (Witness) ________ (Date) ________ (Signature of person receiving child)

________ (Organization — If Applicable)

________ (Address)

Identification of person(s) receiving child:

Driver's license number ________ State ________
Social Security number ________
Other ________

IV. REPORT OF HOSPITAL

________ (Name of Hospital)
________ (Name of Attending Physician)
________ (Mother's Name)
________ (Father's Name)

________ (Address)
________ (Mother's Admission Date) ________ (Discharge Date)
________ (Mother's Address)
________ (Father's Address)
________ (Signature of Administrator or Designated Representative)

See Instructions on reverse side

AD 22 (10/75)

Authorization For Pick Up Of Child

G

AUTHORIZATION FOR PICKING UP CHILD

TO WHOM IT MAY CONCERN:

I/We ______________________ the mother/father of ______________________

child born ______________ at ______________
(birth date) (place)

authorize ______________________________,
(name)

______________________, ______________________
(address)

to remove him/her from the home of ______________________
(name of foster mother or other person)

and to make plans for his care.

____
(Parent's Signature)

Dated ______________ 19__
(month, day, year)

I, ______________________ authorize and empower the person(s) named in Section I hereof to make any provisions for medical and surgical care for my child identified on the face of this report, including anesthesia, which may be deemed necessary or advisable by any licensed physician.

Witness ______________________ ______________________
(Mother)

Dated ______________________ Dated ______________________

Petition

The Petition To Adopt is a form filed by the prospective adoptive parents when they take custody of the child, formally notifying the court of their intent to adopt. Each state varies in the length of the time between petition and finalization, usually from six months to one year.

Petition To Adopt

H

SUPERIOR COURT OF THE STATE OF ....
FOR THE COUNTY OF.......................................

No....................

Adoption of
...., a Minor
(Name of child)

PETITION FOR ADOPTION
JOINED IN BY
ADOPTION AGENCY

1. The petitioners, ..., are husband and wife, residing in the County of................................., State of ...., and desire to adopt..., who was born in
(Names of petitioners) (Name of child)
....on................................., 19........ The petitioners are adult persons, more than ten years older than the above-named minor person.
(Place of birth)

2. ...., being licensed by the State Department of Social Welfare as an adoption agency, placed this child for adoption with the petitioners on ...., 19........, consents to the adoption by them, and joins in this petition.
(Name of adoption agency)

3. ....of the child
(The parent entitled to sole custody/The parents)
....................placed the child directly with the petitioners and.................
(has/have) (is/are)
prepared to consent to the child's adoption by the petitioners.

(Where no parental consent is required)

No consent to adoption by any parent is required by reason of the fact (State facts to bring the case within the exceptions set out in C.C. §224. i.e., (1) parents dead, (2) abandonment decree, (3) parents deserted child without identification, or (4) parents relinquished child to adoption agency.)

4. The child is a proper subject for adoption, the petitioners' home is suitable for the child, and they are able to support and care for the child properly. The interest of the child will be promoted by this adoption. The petitioners agree to treat the child in all respects as their own lawful child.

5. Each petitioner hereby consents to the adoption of the child by the other.

WHEREFORE, petitioners pray that the court adjudge the adoption of the child by petitioners, declaring that each petitioner and the child shall thenceforth sustain toward each other the legal relation of parent and child, and have all the rights and be subject to all the duties of that relation; and that the child shall be known as..
(New name of child)

Dated:..

____
Petitioner

____
Petitioner

____
Attorney for Petitioners

Consent/Surrender/Relinquishment Termination of Parental Rights

In private or independent adoptions, the birthparents sign a consent form that gives permission directly to the adoptive parents to adopt their child. In agency adoptions, birthparents sign a surrender or relinquishment form that gives custody of the child to the agency which, in turn, grants the agency the right to decide who will adopt the child. A court ordered termination of parental rights would occur if the child had been abandoned, neglected or abused and the birthparent refused to relinquish or failed to respond.

Consent To Adopt

IN THE SUPERIOR COURT OF THE STATE OF

IN AND FOR THE COUNTY OF ______________

IN THE MATTER OF THE ADOPTION OF

a Minor

Consent to Adoption by Parent

I, the undersigned, being the mother/father of the above-named minor child, and entitled to the sole custody of the said child, do hereby give my full and free consent to the adoption of said child by

____
Names of petitioners

the petitioners herein, it being fully understood by me that with the signing of this document my consent may not be withdrawn except with court approval and that with the signing of the order of adoption by the court I shall give up all my rights of custody, services, and earnings of said child and that said child cannot be reclaimed by me.

Said child was born on ______________ in ______________
Date / City and State

Date ______________ 19___

____
Signature of Parent

____
Witness to Signature of Parent

Signed in the presence of

____

[SEAL]

Surrender/Relinquishment

RELINQUISHMENT J

I, the ____________ of ______________________________, a minor
We,

________ child, born ____________, ______________________________
sex date city state

do hereby relinquish and surrender said child for adoption to ______________________________

____

an organization licensed by the Department of Health of the State of ________ to find homes for children and to place children in homes for adoption. It is fully understood by me/us that when this relinquishment is filed with the State Department of Health by said agency, all my/our rights to the custody, services, and earnings of said minor child and any responsibilty for the care and support of said minor child will be terminated and that said child cannot be reclaimed by me/us.

____

____

The foregoing instrument was signed on ______________________________ by the said ____
date

______________________________ in the presence of us, who have signed the same as witnesses thereto.

____

____

STATE OF
ss.
County of ____________

On this ____ day of ____________; 19____, before me, ______________________________
______________________________ an authorized official of the
______________________________, an organization licensed by the Department of Health of the State of ________ to find homes for children and place them in homes for adoption, personally appeared ______________________________
____
known to me to be the person(s) whose name(s) is/are subscribed to the within instrument and acknowledged to me that he/she/they executed the same.

____
Authorized Official of Agency

____
Title

Interlocutory

In some states an interlocutory decree is issued between the time of relinquishment and the petition, stipulating custody. Other states do not issue this document.

Final Decree

When the court has reviewed the petition and all supporting data, and has determined the adoption to be in the child's best interests, it will issue a final decree. All parties should request a copy for their files. This is the legal document that permanently transfers parental rights, responsibilites and custody

(Title of Court) K

(Title of Cause)

No....................

JUDGMENT OF ADOPTION

The petition of..for an order of this
(Names of petitioners)
Court adjudging that henceforth......................................, a minor, shall
(Name of child)
be the adopted child of the petitioners came on regularly this day for hearing, ...appearing as attorney for the
(Name of attorney)
petitioners; and the petitioners and the child having appeared before the Court, and the Court having examined them, each separately; and the Court having heard the petition and evidence in support thereof, and the matter being submitted, the Court finds:

1. That all the averments contained in the petition of........................
(Names
....are true; that they are husband and wife,
of petitioners)
and each has consented to the adoption of this child by the other; that each of them is an adult person, and is more than ten years older than the unmarried minor;

2. That each parent whose consent is required by law has consented, in the manner and form prescribed, to the adoption of the child by the petitioners herein, and each consent has been filed with the clerk of this Court; and that the Department of Social Welfare or the county adoption agency has filed herein its acceptance of said consents and its report setting forth the legal status of the child;

3. That the petitioners have executed an agreement that the child shall be treated in all respects as the lawful child of petitioners, and each of them;

4. That the child is a proper subject for adoption, and the petitioners' home is suitable for the child; and that the interests of the child will be promoted by his adoption by the petitioners; now, therefore,

IT IS ORDERED that..be adopted by
(Name of child)
...., husband and wife, and that these
(Names of petitioners)
persons shall hereafter sustain toward each other all legal obligations of parent and child, and shall have all the rights and be under all of the duties of such relationship, including all legal rights and duties of custody, support, and inheritance.

IT IS FURTHER ORDERED that the child shall hereafter bear the family name of petitioners, and shall be known as..
(New name of child)

Dated:..

Judge

Final Decree

Final Decree

Judgment — Adoption — Chambers. K

STATE OF MINNESOTA, DISTRICT COURT,

8752

COUNTY OF HENNEPIN, FOURTH JUDICIAL DISTRICT.

In the matter of the petition of

Gen Roy G. Webster and
Helen R. Webster, his wife JUDGMENT AND DECREE

For the adoption of December 15, 1949
Anita Marie Leech

A MINOR CHILD.

The above entitled matter came regularly on for hearing before the above named court, at Chambers, on the 15th day of Dec. A. D. 19 49 ; and the court being fully advised in the premises, did, on the 15th day of Dec. A. D. 1949 , duly make and file its order granting the prayer of the petitioner herein.

Now, pursuant to said order and on motion of O'Neill J. Gwathmel, Esquire Attorney for petitioners it is hereby adjudged and decreed that from and after the date hereof, said child, Anita Marie Leech shall be deemed and taken to be the child and heir of the petitioners above named in all respects the same as though born to them in lawful wedlock.

It is further adjudged and decreed that the name of said child be, and the same is hereby changed from that of Anita Marie Leech to Mary Jo Webster

By the Court: B. K. WASMUTH,
Clerk of District Court.
By
Deputy.

Birth Certificates

ORIGINAL BIRTH CERTIFICATE

Each state varies according to its access to vital records but in most states either parent can request a certified copy of the original certificate of birth after it has been filed with the county and state. Both the birth and adoptive parents should obtain two certified copies and keep one for their own files and one for the adoptee's. Hospitals often issue a birth certificate, which though nice to have, is not a certified copy. The original certificate of birth must be ordered before finalization of the adoption if the record is to be sealed and an amended certificate filed in its place.

Original Birth Certificate Request Letter

L

Bureau of Vital Statistics
State Department of Health
Address
City, State, Zip

Dear Registrar;

Please search for and provide a LONG FORM copy of the record of birth of my son/daughter:

NAME: (Name given at birth) (or Baby Boy/Girl Surname)
BORN: (Month/Day/Year)
(City/County/State)
MOTHER: (Birthmother's name at time of child's birth)
FATHER: (Birthfather's name)

A MONEY ORDER FOR $________ is enclosed.

Sincere appreciation for any endeavor you extend to this request.

Name
Street
City, State, Zip

Original Birth Certificate

M

CERTIFICATE OF LIVE BIRTH

STATE BIRTH CERTIFICATE NUMBER — LOCAL REGISTRATION DISTRICT AND CERTIFICATE NUMBER

THIS CHILD	1A. NAME OF CHILD—FIRST: Karen	1B. MIDDLE: Anne	1C. LAST: Lindsey
	2. SEX: F	3A. THIS BIRTH—SINGLE, TWIN, ETC.: Single	5A. DATE OF BIRTH—MONTH, DAY, YEAR: September 28, 1953 — 5B. HOUR: 9:40 a.m.
PLACE OF BIRTH	6A. PLACE OF BIRTH—NAME OF HOSPITAL: Memorial	6B. STREET ADDRESS: 622 North Street	
	6C. CITY OR TOWN: Charlestown	6D. COUNTY: Croix	
MOTHER OF CHILD	7A. BIRTH NAME OF MOTHER—FIRST: Katherina	7B. MIDDLE: Anne	7C. LAST: Lindsey — 8. STATE OF BIRTH: Vermont — 9. AGE OF MOTHER: 19
FATHER OF CHILD	10A. NAME OF FATHER—FIRST: Darren	10B. MIDDLE:	10C. LAST: Brown — 11. STATE OF BIRTH: Florida — 12. AGE OF FATHER: 22
PARENT'S CERTIFICATION		13A. PARENT OR OTHER INFORMANT—SIGNATURE: Karen T Lindsey	13B. RELATIONSHIP TO CHILD: mother — 13C. DATE: Oct 1, 1953
ATTENDANT'S CERTIFICATION		14A. PHYSICIAN—SIGNATURE: [signature] — 14C. ADDRESS: 155 Michigan Avenue Charlestown	14B. DATE SIGNED: 10/1/53 — 14D. ATTENDANT'S LICENSE NUMBER: 8027634264
LOCAL REGISTRAR	15. DEATH—ENTER DATE OF DEATH	16. LOCAL REGISTRAR—SIGNATURE: Rosalind Burns	17. DATE ACCEPTED FOR REGISTRATION: Oct 25, 1953

CONFIDENTIAL INFORMATION FOR PUBLIC HEALTH USE ONLY

FATHER	19. RACE: Caucasian	20. ETHNICITY: Swedish	21A. USUAL OCCUPATION: Mechanic	21B. KIND OF BUSINESS OR INDUSTRY: Airlines
MOTHER	23. RACE: Caucasian	24. ETHNICITY: German	25A. USUAL OCCUPATION: Student	25B. KIND OF BUSINESS OR INDUSTRY:
	26A. RESIDENCE: 18 Main Avenue		26B. CITY OR TOWN: Charlestown	26C.
	26D. COUNTY: Croix	26E. STATE:	27. PREGNANCY HISTORY	
MEDICAL DATA	28A. DATE LAST NORMAL MENSES BEGAN: January 1, 1953	28B. MONTH OF PREGNANCY PRENATAL CARE BEGAN: 3rd	29. BIRTHWEIGHT: 6lbs 7 oz.	LIVE BIRTHS: Now living 0, Now dead 0 — OTHER TERMINATIONS: 0, 0
	ENTER THE APPROPRIATE CODE OR CODES FOR EACH ITEM 32 THRU 35 FROM THE VS 10A SUPPLEMENTAL WORKSHEET. IF NONE ENTER—NONE.			DATE OF LAST LIVE BIRTH: – — DATE OF LAST TERMINATION: –
	32. COMPLICATIONS OF PREGNANCY AND CONCURRENT ILLNESSES: None			
	33A. COMPLICATIONS OF LABOR AND DELIVERY: None	33B. CAESAREAN SECTION: None	34. BIRTH INJURY TO CHILD: None	35. CONGENITAL MALFORMATION: None
STATE REGISTRAR	A.	B.	C.	D. E. F.

NOTICE: THE INFORMATION YOU PROVIDE IN COMPLETING THE BOTTOM HALF OF THE BIRTH CERTIFICATE WILL BE KEPT STRICTLY CONFIDENTIAL AND WILL BE USED FOR HEALTH AND MEDICAL PURPOSES ONLY.

AMENDED CERTIFICATE

After an adoption has been finalized an amended birth certificate may be filed. As stated before, preferably this would not eliminate access to the original or delete any of the birthfamily information, but only add adoptive family information. If that does not happen, each parent should order a certified copy of the amended certificate several weeks after filing.

Amended Birth Certificate — Unpreferrable

CERTIFICATE OF LIVE BIRTH N

THIS CHILD	Doris	Lorraine	McCutchen
	F	Single	September 28, 1953 — 9:40 a.m.
PLACE OF BIRTH	Charlestown		Croix
MOTHER OF CHILD	Helen	Lorraine	Duffy — Texas — 32
FATHER OF CHILD	George	Harold	McCutchen — Oklahoma — 37
PARENT'S CERTIFICATION			
ATTENDANT'S CERTIFICATION	Dr. O.J. Olsen		10/1/53
	155 Michigan Avenue Charlestown		Q7776342-64
LOCAL REGISTRAR	Rosalind Burns		10/25/53

CONFIDENTIAL INFORMATION FOR PUBLIC HEALTH USE ONLY

FATHER | MOTHER | MEDICAL DATA

ENTER THE APPROPRIATE CODE OR CODES FOR EACH ITEM 32 THRU 35 FROM THE VS 10A SUPPLEMENTAL WORKSHEET. IF NONE ENTER—NONE.

STATE REGISTRAR | A. | B. | C. | D. | E. | F.

NOTICE: THE INFORMATION YOU PROVIDE IN COMPLETING THE BOTTOM HALF OF THE BIRTH CERTIFICATE WILL BE KEPT STRICTLY CONFIDENTIAL AND WILL BE USED FOR HEALTH AND MEDICAL PURPOSES ONLY.

Adoption Certificate — Preferrable

O

CERTIFICATE OF ADOPTION

STATE DEPARTMENT OF HEALTH
DIVISION OF VITAL STATISTICS

PART I — Adopting parents must furnish the following information as it relates to them at the TIME OF BIRTH of the child.

NATURAL OR ADOPTIVE FATHER

First Name of Father / Middle / Last: George Harold McCutchen

Date of Birth: 12/2/1916 — Birthplace (State, Country): Oklahoma — Race or Color: Caucasian — Usual Occupation: General Manager — Kind of Business or Industry: Textiles

NATURAL OR ADOPTIVE MOTHER

First Maiden Name of Mother / Middle / Last: Helen Lorraine Duffy

Date of Birth: 2/23/1921 — Birthplace (State, Country): Texas — Race or Color: Caucasian — Present Mailing Address of Adopting Parents: 222 Circle Drive Charlestown

Usual Residence (City or Town, County and State at the Time of Birth of Child): Charlestown, Croix County — Residence Located Inside City Limits ___ Yes X No — Residence Located On a Farm ___ Yes ___ No

Was Adoptive Father the Natural Father ___ Yes X No — Was Adoptive Mother the Natural Mother ___ Yes X No — Is the Adoption by Only One Person ___ Yes X No

ATTORNEY OR AGENCY HANDLING CASE

Name of Attorney or Agency Handling Case: Phil Miller

Mailing Address: 16 Main Street Suite 643 . Charlestown

PART II — This information must be given as of the date of birth.

CHILD'S PERSONAL DATA

First Name of Child at Birth / Middle / Last: Karen Anne Lindsey Brown

Sex: F — Date of Birth: September 28, 1953 — Place of Birth (City or Town, County, State): Charlestown, Croix County — Race or Color: Caucasian

Was Place of Birth Hospital or Institution X Yes ___ No — If Born in Hospital or Institution, Give Name of Hospital or Institution: Memorial

NATURAL PARENTS' DATA

Name of Natural Father: Darren William Brown 3/10/1931 Florida Mechanic Airlines

Maiden Name of Natural Mother: Katherina Anne Lindsey 4/1/1934 Vermont Student

PART III — To be completed by the Circuit Clerk and sent to the State Registrar.

I Hereby Certify that the Child Described Above Was Adopted by the Above Parent(s) on This Date, and is Now to Bear the Name of: Doris Lorraine Karen Anne Lindsey Brown McCutchen — As Set Forth in the Decree of Adoption, Order Number: A005349

Circuit Clerk in and for the County of: Croix — State of

Signature and Seal of Circuit Clerk: *Robert E. Paulsen* — Date Signed: *Dec. 12, 1954*

CERTIFICATION OF STATE REGISTRAR

I Hereby Certify that This Adoption Information Was Received on This Date: *DECEMBER 20, 1954* — *Rosalind Burns* —State Registrar

Audio Visual Records

Photographs, audio cassette tapes, video tapes and films can provide wonderful memory albums for all parties involved and especially for the adoptee. Remember, the adoptee may not have any conscious or clear memory of those events and the more visual and audio aids where (s)he can see and hear him/herself the better. These can be root, continuity and foundation forming tools. Some extended families have video taped and photographed the pregnancy progression and the birth. Others have recorded the first visits after the child's birth. And still others have the court finalization on record. Adoption should be a celebrated expansion of everyone's lives, relationships and experience. Recording those moments reinforces that celebration.

A *Memory Album* would be a good joint effort for both the adoptive and birth families. Each can provide photographs of their lives and histories and the *Memory Album* can be their joint gift to the adoptee. Don't edit each other in this endeavor. Each should add things as (s)he sees fit.

If you choose audio cassette tapes as one way to record the event, make sure that you have good quality tapes, recorder and microphone. These tapes must last for a lifetime. You might want to record each meeting between prospective birth and adoptive families. You might want to record the meetings with social workers and attorneys. Think in terms of the child's heritage and inquisitiveness. Not every child will have intense interest in these efforts, but don't prejudge that for him/her.

Written records and audio cassettes are efficient and easy but make sure you supplement them with visuals. Photographs are easiest and preserve the best. Film and video tape are great too! Just remember to keep all these things stored well, as time tends to make them fade and heat destroys them.

For interracial and intercountry adoptions it can be additionally beneficial to have the visual and audio tools to assist in the child's development and cultural identity.

Putting It All Together

Accumulating all these documents, records and thoughts can be mind boggling. Let us recommend a chronological order that can be added to as ongoing relationships and events become recorded. A filing system, photo album, looseleaf notebook, and/or journal are all useful ways of organizing the data. Here is a check list of the things you may want to include:

- ☐ PHOTOS OF PREGNANCY
- ☐ PHOTOS OF BIRTHFAMILY HISTORY
- ☐ PHOTOS OF ADOPTIVE FAMILY HISTORY
- ☐ PHOTOS OF FIRST MEETING
- ☐ NOTES OF FIRST MEETING BY ALL PARENTS
- ☐ AUDIO CASSETTE RECORDINGS OF FIRST MEETING
- ☐ VIDEO CASSETTE/FILM OF FIRST MEETING
- ☐ PHOTOS OF SUBSEQUENT MEETINGS
- ☐ NOTES OF SUBSEQUENT MEETINGS BY ALL PARTICIPANTS
- ☐ AUDIO CASSETTE RECORDINGS OF SUBSEQUENT MEETINGS
- ☐ VIDEO CASSETTE/FILM OF SUBSEQUENT MEETINGS
- ☐ PHOTOS OF HOSPTIAL/BIRTH
- ☐ NOTES OF HOSPITAL/BIRTH BY ALL PARTICIPATING FAMILY
- ☐ AUDIO CASSETTE RECORDINGS OF BIRTH/HOSPITAL
- ☐ VIDEO CASSETTE/FILM OF BIRTH/HOSPITAL
- ☐ HOSPITAL RECORDS
- ☐ PHOTOS OF FIRST TIME CHILD IS WITH ADOPTIVE FAMILY
- ☐ NOTES OF FIRST TIME CHILD IS WITH ADOPTIVE FAMILY BY ALL PARTICIPANTS
- ☐ AUDIO/VIDEO/FILM OF FIRST TIME CHILD IS WITH ADOPTIVF FAMILY
- ☐ ORIGINAL CERTIFICATE OF BIRTH
- ☐ ALL PARENTS' MEDICAL HISTORIES
- ☐ PHOTOS OF CUSTODY TRANSFER AND COURT
- ☐ NOTES OF CUSTODY TRANSFER AND COURT
- ☐ AUDIO/VIDEO/FILM RECORDING OF CUSTODY TRANSFER AND COURT
- ☐ MEDICAL CONSENT
- ☐ INTERLOCUTORY
- ☐ ADOPTION PETITION
- ☐ CASE FILES
- ☐ HOME STUDY
- ☐ CONSENT TO ADOPT/RELINQUISHMENT/TERMINATION
- ☐ FINAL DECREE
- ☐ ATTORNEYS/DOCTORS/COURT/AGENCIES/FOSTER CARE RECORDS
- ☐ LETTERS/TAPES MADE FOR THE CHILD
- ☐ AMENDED BIRTH CERTIFICATE.

Ideally, you would want to have all these things for your child. But, of course, you must pick and choose what all of you are comfortable with and able to do. Though you are doing this to guarantee your child's access to both families and to the information (s)he may desire about him/herself, you are also doing this for you. If you can truly celebrate this event and joyously participate and share the other parents' emotional hills and valleys, you will have added to everyone's life. Adoption does not have to be loss or gain oriented, it can be an event that is seen as an extension of life's options for everyone involved. Remember, in a cooperative adoption EVERYONE WINS.

SECTION IV

COOPERATIVE FAMILIES

Families

Over the last two years we have seen several simple characteristics prominent in the families who are in touch with us. It seems that those people who choose cooperative adoptions function with a strong faith and belief system. They believe in the integrity of others, in themselves and often have strong religious and spiritual connections. Over and over again we have seen these families confront minor conflict or major crisis by coming together rather than pulling apart. They recognize each others capabilities and weaknesses and are not critical but constructive in their discussions. We have never seen them demean or belittle each other even when feeling great pressure.

Not all their families or friends understand or are supportive of their extended family relationships, but somehow they have the strength and commitment to continue. Many have said they just know it feels right. Though these relationships are sometimes a struggle, the glow of joy and well-being that emanates when they are together reinforces their families. As you will see in the photos and stories that follow, these people are as individual and varied as the rest of society. They come from all backgrounds, but they all have decided there is benefit to adding family and options to their childrens' lives.

There are several elements not included in these stories. Though many birthfathers and families with intercountry placements are involved we had not yet received stories from them at the time of publication. There is also the omission of the adoptee speaking for his/herself. As time goes on, and the children involved in cooperative adoptions mature, we will hear them speak for themselves.

If you have further interest in knowing more about Cooperative Adoption or about specific families and how they work, there are many audio, video tapes and support groups available. (See Appendix)

PHOTO BY BARRY SLOBIN

Adam and Nathan

Nathan, Adam and Birthmom, Jeri

Birthmother, Jeri; Adam; Birth grandpa, Mike, and grandma Nita; Nathan and adoptive mom, Eileen

Adoptive Dad, Steve holds Adam and Nathan as birth grand mother, Nita feeds them.

PHOTOS BY BARRY SLOBIN

The Frees and The Langes, An Extended Family

Adoptive Mom, Eileen; Birthmom, Jeri; and their twin boys, Nathan and Adam

PHOTOS BY BARRY SLOBIN

A Love Story

We Had A Pregnant Teenager

By Nita Jo Frees

Our normally vivacious and bubbly daughter, Jeri, came into our kitchen on her lunch hour from High School in a state of pain and inward agony of soul that ripped one apart to watch. After pleading again and again for an explanation, she haltingly responded with words I never thought I would hear. "Mom,....I'm so ashamed. ....Mom, ...I'm pregnant!"

My mind and emotions went wild. Every part of my being went into a shock reaction. My heart pounded so hard I could hardly believe it did not burst out of my body. Eventually, I moaned out, "Who?"

She told me who and I asked "When? How far along are you?"

"Late December. I'm seventeen weeks along."

Our daughter had carried the fear of thinking and rejecting the idea she was pregnant for three and one-half months. Oh yes, I had suspected it could be an answer to why she was eating so much and sleeping all the time. She had gained weight in "pregnant areas". My mind could be logical, but it was much better at rejecting the whole idea. Jeri was a "good" girl. She had been in a church all her life. No, she could not be pregnant. But reality was now upon us. She *was* pregnant and we had to deal with her and a precious life growing under her ribs.

Jeri was sixteen and in her junior year of high school when all this happened. She was planning on going to college to become a teacher. Suddenly, she had to face mature decisions that would effect her and the baby the rest of their lives. The incredible pain we were in was only for a season. The decisions Jeri had to make were for life.

We talked and cried all afternoon. "Jeri," I asked "What do you plan to do?"

"I think I want to put the baby up for adoption." answered Jeri.

"Does the father know you are pregnant?" (They had only seen each other once after the conception.)

"Yes, I think so." Jeri answered, "I called him a long time ago and told him I thought I was pregnant. I've tried to call him, but I cannot get hold of him."

"Will he go along with adoption?"

"Oh, I think so. He doesn't want any part of this. He felt badly, but he is really scared."

We talked a great deal about adoption and about all the hardships that keeping the baby could bring on her and us. We discussed how unfair it could be to the baby to be raised in such a situation and how wonderful adoption might be for a couple that had infertility problems. We totally agreed on adoption, but we did not want a secret one.

Jeri's father came home and I choked out the news after making him sit down. Mike and Jeri had been at odds for about three years. They fought and bickered all the time over nothing. But now when his "little girl" needed love, he had a heart as big as could be found. Now, I could face whatever was in the future. We were together as a family.

We talked long into the night. One decision was to not hide Jeri in any way. We went straight to the church and told the pastor. I told my adult Sunday School class. Jeri went to the youth group and told them. Because of this openness we had love instead of criticism and gossip. We asked for help and we got it in abundance.

The next step was the doctor and professional care for Jeri. Within one week we were able to watch *TWINS* frolicking under Jeri's ribs. Twins posed a week long re-evaluation of the adoption decision. We all realized that if one baby to raise was too much for Jeri, two surely would be. We would still try to learn about adoption.

We then began a most shocking few months of phone calls. Out of the air would come a call regarding the twins from childless couples. They were so frantic and expectant that we might be able to bring joy to their lives. We had made contact with a christian service and were doing everything through them. One strong desire was for the adoption to be legal. We would refer the calls to the service. We were made painfully aware of the suffering of childless couples with each desperate call.

Before long we were poring over ten files of couples, trying to decide the right couple for Jeri's twins. We saw pictures. We read resumes. We were a part of the whole process. We were choosing the life long Mother and Father of the twins. We could not provide the home they would need, but we wanted the most perfect home possible in our place. We had two "maybe's" in the ten files, then finally found the couple that was *THE COUPLE* without a doubt in our minds.

Three days later we learned, with squeals of delight, that our couple had agreed to the twins. After one month and several letters we met. It was love at first sight. They brought gifts for Jeri and us. The next day Jeri received a big bouquet of flowers. Jeri already knew she was important, not just the two babies growing inside her. We realized that the decision for adoption was definitely the wisest choice.

Eileen and Steve, the adopting parents, voiced a strong desire to be a part of the birth process. We had not considered it, but all readily agreed. Eileen came to our home weekly for the Child Birthing Classes and spent the night. Jeri was put in bed for the last eight weeks of pregnancy. Since we were on vacation one of those weeks, Eileen stayed and cared for her. She got to experience "her" pregnancy and the care of her twins by caring for Jeri. They had a wonderful time getting truly acquainted.

At about 10:30 a.m. I was awakened to, "Mom I'm in so much pain."

I bolted out of bed. I asked dumb questions and got more scared with the answers. Finally, we called the doctor. He said he did not understand the pain, but to get her to the hospital. He arrived thirty minutes later to announce, "Get the delivery room ready. She is at full dilation." By now the strange pain was hard, hard labor.

We called to get Steve and Eileen heading north. They did not make the birth, but were in time to see Jeri rolled out of recovery. Somehow, they had a huge bouquet of long stemmed red roses waiting for her. She dearly loves flowers.

They would go to see her, tell her how wonderful the babies were, then back they would go to their baby sons. We were all together for five days, so excited and comfortable with each other. The hospital staff and doctors did not understand our openness at all. They were overly cautious of Jeri. Nothing we could say or do would help them understand. (We now have them calling us about adoption problems! They could see how healthy it was for all of us.)

The final separation was not easy. In fact, it still is a tender spot in our emotions. We had grown to love Eileen and Steve. Eileen, Mike, Jeri and I had talked for weeks about the future. Steve was not able to come weekly, so he had missed our talks. We realized we did not want separation day to be the end of our Cooperative Adoption. We had cared for Jeri and maintained the happiest home and atmosphere possible for the babies. She had never once done anything to jeopardize their health, which included the adult decision for a C-Section to protect them. We loved them dearly.

Up to the point of birth, Steve and Eileen were asking their hearts desire. Now we were expressing ours. Would it be possible to remain in their lives? We were all so comfortable with each other. They knew and trusted that Jeri would never demand the babies back. She had made a commitment to them. We did have one future time to count on. We planned to all be a part of the Dedication Service of Adam and Nathan.

The three months that intervened were a time of hell and healing. We felt so empty. We went around like zombies in a daze. Jeri had to get over surgery and tackle her senior year of High School. School had started before she delivered. The school could not have been more supportive.

Eileen would write and send us pictures. The letters would cheer us and help us realize how happy she and Steve were. We also could realize how well the twins were doing. The pictures confirmed it all. We would almost wear the pictures out looking at them. They were and still are so very healing.

As Steve and Eileen began to relax in their parenthood, we began to see more and more of them. We are all one big, happy, family now. The twins have three sets of grandparents and two Mommies. For the most part, Jeri will just be Jeri, but when the first opportunity comes to help Adam and Nathan understand her important role in their lives, it will be done. The whole adoption has been a type of wooing and courting. We all have learned to love in a far greater way. Not only were Mike, Jeri's brother and I challenged to love her even more in the midst of a real trauma, but we expanded that love to add two more "children" (Steve and Eileen) and two grandchildren to our family. We have camped together, kept the twins while Steve and Eileen recharge, celebrated holidays and visted often. We've stretched the term "open" to its fullest definition and are ready to keep right on stretching whenever possible.

The twins are now fourteen months old. We still deal with pain, but seeing the joy and experiencing the love of our adopted family far out-weighs the pain. I would not want to have to go through this again, but if we did, I would do it the same way. Many have said our adoption is unique because it has so much love and contact. I agree, but also wonder if people involved in adoption should not look at it and sincerely consider at least getting to know each other. Despite everyone's fears, our mixed lives were not threats, they were healing for all of us. We all leaned heavily on our faith in God. He lead us down a brave, new path and took our feelings of tragedy, and brought great blessing to us all.

Welcome To The Family

By Steve and Eileen Lange

Our story is a love story. Our love is not just for our adopted twin boys, Adam and Nathan. They have brought us unspeakable joy. It is also for the incredible opportunity to love their natural mother and family. We have shocked our family and friends with this unusual relationship. Yet, we believe it is exactly what our God would have us do.

Love at first sight is precisely what we felt the first time we saw our babies birth mother, Jeri. Of course, it was the first time we were able to feast our eyes on the sight of our expected twins. Jeri was only six months along, but she was huge.

We all believe that it has been our common faith and trust in God that has brought us to this degree of openness and cooperation. We were able to defy the walls of secrecy and shame that so often surround adoption. We feel we have been an example to countless others caught in the web of untimely pregnancy or infertility.

There were never any preconceived notions or agreements about on-going contact after the birth between the natural family and our family except for one. Jeri and her family desired earnestly to be present at the babies' Church Dedication. After that first visit, we knew something special was about to take place.

Part of the "falling in love" process took place in the two and one-half months preceding birth. I visited the birth family weekly to encourage Jeri and attend the Birthing Classes. Because of the great distance, I would spend the night. This gave me the opportunity to be with the babies and experience pregnancy second-hand. We would often express our feelings and desires about the adoption. Never did we make demands on one another. Often desires and concerns would surface without any solution. Although this was frustrating to all, it helped us to become patient and develop unconditional love. An example of this was my desire to be in the room at birth. Jeri and family felt it was no problem. The doctors could not agree. We wanted it so badly, but we all had to wait for the answer.

Another facet of our love story was that the birth family felt genuine joy for us and our new babies. On the other hand we could sympathize with their grief. It was mutually sensitive relationship. When we returned home from the hospital with our two bundles of joy there was a sadness in our hearts and a feeling of real ambivalence. We had great joy at what was in our arms and great loss over the special bond that had developed during the last trimester of Jeri's pregnancy. Our hearts were leaning one way, yet everyone around us cautioned us against becoming too close. It seems that the constant cautioning and misunderstanding are the biggests risks of contact with the natural family.

We often stop to contemplate the tremendous gifts God has given us through Jeri and her willingness for Adam and Nathan to have a secure home with two parents. It is not hard to admire and love both her and her family for that brave commitment. In a time where abortion is common, it would have been a less incriminating option. Instead, she chose life and the joy in giving that life and sharing with a couple who could not have children naturally.

Although we regularly communicated in letters it was not until the boys were almost two months old that Jeri was invited over. This was a big test for all of us, with many lessons to learn as a result. First, there was the lesson of introducing Jeri to a houseful of friends who were visiting. She had always been most honest about introducing us as the adoptive mother and father. We felt she deserved the same type of honesty. So we introduced her to our friends as the boys' natural mother. Next, it was watching her reaction to Adam and Nathan. It was absolutely painless and priceless at the same time. There were no fears— just joy at how much they had changed and how well they were doing. The third lesson was in watching the reactions of some very dear friends as they participated in the whole situation. There was genuine fear and concern over this type of contact— even from people we loved dearly. They could not feel our peace and trust. We are pleased to say that for the most part this fear has greatly diminshed. We believe people can sense our joy and comfort now.

We have gone camping, water skiing, snow skiing and just visiting with our extended family. People marvel at how we manage. We feel just as much a part of the birth family as we feel Adam and Nathan are a part of our family.

There was a real time of questioning the appropriateness of all this contact. Had we met the family elsewhere and under different circumstances than adoption, we would have felt most comfortable with them in our lives. The fact that we share in the love of Adam and Nathan only enhances the bond of love. People would accept the first form of love, but the adoption was suppose to make a difference.

We have gone away on several weekend vacations and have left the boys with their birth grandparents. It is a blessing to see how much this trust means to the birth family. My own parents have just returned from spending a weekend visiting them for an early extended family Thanksgiving. There is so much love that we feel this cannot possibly hurt the boys. It will give them a firm foundation.

The birth grandparents will be called grandparents. The boys also have a set of birth great-grandparents. Jeri will be Jeri for the time being, but it is our desire that Adam and Nathan will always know that she is their birthmother. It is also our hope that at some point in their lives they will also call her ''Mother''. We can never and would never deny who she is. We are grateful for who she is and what she has added to our lives. This is not out of obligation, but out of love and deep respect.

Steve's parents are not at all comfortable with our relationship. They feel we are going to be confusing the boys. They think it is selfish of the birth family to desire contact. There is little research to rely on for this type of situation. We are content with our new family. It has been hard to deal with the lack of support from Steve's parents. On the other hand, it is understandable. An adoption with contact was unknown in their generation. Their fear is based on that upbringing.

We have chosen a different path. It is one which we believe will provide a healthy self-concept for our children. They will never have to wonder who or where their birth mother is. They will always know her. They will not need to worry about deception and dishonesty from us, because we will always tell them the truth. They will never have to "search" for their roots. They will be attached to them.

In return for the delight of raising two babies, we did not believe this contact was too much to be asked for from us. In fact, we feel it is essential.

**A full length book "We Have Two Mommies" telling of this cooperative adoption and the concepts learned in the process is pending publication at this time. (See Appendix).*

PHOTO BY MARTIN BRANDFON

Colleen D Houlihan and daughters. Dara is on the right.

The Story Of Dara

By Tricia Hagen

In January, 1979 I was 4 months pregnant. Until that point I had planned to have the baby and raise it myself. I had even begun to buy baby clothes and plan for the future. I chose this solution because I didn't feel that there were any other alternatives. I could not be satisfied with the traditional agency adoption. It was totally unacceptable to me and I wasn't sure it would be healthy for my child either. I knew I couldn't leave my baby with strangers, never knowing where she was, and I could not tolerate the possibility that she could grow up thinking I didn't love her.

I was approached in February by a good friend with a different solution. She told me that her sister-in-law Colleen, and Colleen's husband Jim were unable to have children and had been trying to adopt. They were interested in a private, open adoption. I had been assured that there would be an open relationship between Colleen, Jim, and me and my child, and that my child would be raised in an open, loving environment encouraging trust and honesty. It seemed to be an ideal approach and one I could be comfortable with.

Soon afterwards I flew to California with a very close friend. She was to be my labor coach. We both stayed with Colleen and Jim and attended Lamaze classes in preparation for the birth. My daughter, Dara was born on June 9th at 2:31 a.m. after more than 20 hours of labor. She went home at noon of the same day and my friend and I stayed in a hotel for a few days before returning to Wisconsin.

I have had continued contact with Dara and her new family over the last five years. They have been back to Wisconsin three or four times for visits and we have sent letters and pictures back and forth. Now that Dara is older she writes to me herself. I receive beautiful drawings and paintings and short notes thanking me for letters or gifts and telling me she loves me. She can never know how much these things mean to me. I will treasure them the rest of my life. I also have a large photo album filled with pictures that Colleen has sent and I have taken during the visits. I am developing a wonderful relationship with Dara little by little over the years. She is a bright, extremely well-adjusted child, and seems to take for granted the extra set of parents, grandparents, etc. I really feel she is being taught very positive attitudes about her own unique family structure. She does not see being an adoptee as negative because she is not subjected to an atmostphere of secrecy and lies. She is being allowed to benefit from the love of everyone connected to her without having to suffer from misconceptions and destructive prejudices.

I feel cooperative adoption is very beneficial to all involved. There seems to be a much higher incidence of emotional problems in adopted children, and I really feel that much of that can be bypassed with openness and cooperation. In an open, cooperative adoption, the children can have a stronger and more secure sense of identity. They know who they look like and where they came from. They also know that their birthparents did love them and that was why they were placed for adoption, not because their birthparents didn't care.

This has been the best possible solution for Dara and I. Although I don't want to give the impression that this hasn't been painful for me. I have suffered a loss, that is, the loss of my daughter, and I will live with that the rest of my life. That is a fact that will not change, and will not go away no matter what my relationship with Dara is. I will relive that separation every time I see a picture of her, on her birthday or a holiday, and I will feel sad that I can't spend that time with her. But I also feel great joy that I can watch her grow and have an opportunity to develop a relationship with her. I have given her life and a foundation built on her heritage. Colleen and Jim are giving her nurturing and guidance on which to build her life. Together we are giving her love and honesty so that she can be a complete person.

The Story Of Dara

By Colleen D. Houlihan-adoptive mom

In the winter of 1975 my husband, Jim, and I had been married one and one-half years when we decided it wat time to have a baby. After trying for a year, we had all the fertility tests — no problems were found, all the tests were negative — but still no pregnancy.

This was an incredibly frustrating experience since medically, there was no diagnosed problem, and consequently there was no treatment that could be prescribed. We kept trying for another year and finally decided to pursue adoption.

We went to the county adoptions department in the spring of 1978 and finished our Home Study in the fall. We were told it might be three or four years before a baby came to us.

In February 1979 my mother called from Wisconsin, asking if we were still interested in adoption. My brothers' wife had a friend who was pregnant and wanted a private adoption. YES! We shouted!

After several phone calls, including one from me to the birthmothers' mother to reassure her we weren't planning to buy her daughters' baby, Tricia (the birthmother) and her friend, Sue, flew out from Wisconsin in early April. We expected the baby May 1.

We went to birth classes together as Tricia wanted natural childbirth.

Dara was born on June 9, over a month late, at 2:30 a.m. We brought her home at noon. We attended her birth, providing sandwiches and sodas to Sue who was the birth coach and encouragement to Tricia who had a 20 hour labor. Tricia and Sue stayed at a hotel for three days after Dara's birth and then flew home to Wisconsin.

We had no further contact with Tricia until Christmas of that year, when Dara was 6 months old. We visited my family who live in the same town Tricias' family does. Tricia visited with us and took Dara over to meet her birthgrandparents and aunts and to see her birthfather. We also met Bob, Dara's birthfather, who was a friend of Tricias' but no longer a lover. He is a congenial, humorous fellow, but not ready for responsibility. Meeting him reconfirmed my trust in Tricias' decision to relinquish their baby for adoption.

Tricia has sent letters and an occasional present to Dara, and we have sent letters and pictures.

We visited again when Dara was about two and in the summer of 1983 when she was four. This time was a bit different because in the months prior, Dara had asked "whose uterus she grew in". This question was precipitated by my unexpected pregnancy and birth of Bridgid in June of 1982. In discussing reproduction the question had come up. Dara had been told the truth — she grew in the uterus of "our friend Tricia". Her response to this portentious announcement was — "Well, if she ever invites us to her house, can I go so I can see what she looks like?"

I was astonished my three year old would ask that question. I'd heard many adoptees speak of wanting to know who they looked like, but I hadn't realized how important this might be to a three year old child. Luckily we had pictures to show her and she was pleased and satisfied to see her resemblance to Tricia pointed out.

So meeting Tricia again that summer was different. I felt anxious, anticipating deep, significant questions. We all met at our big family 4th of July reunion picnic and it took Dara awhile to get clear who exactly WAS Tricia, with a couple dozen aunts, uncles and cousins around! She stayed overnight with Tricia, who was staying with my brother and his wife. Dara's significant comments on the occasion were about the ice cream they'd had, the biggest swing in the world they had in their yard, Aunti Lynn's goats, and Uncle Sean's treehouse.

This past Christmas Tricia sent Dara a Strawberry Shortcake nightgown and shirt, and asked if Dara had a Cabbage Patch doll. If not she wanted to send her one. She said since the doll came with adoption papers and birth certificate I could use it perhaps to explain to Dara the actual process of adoption.

Tricias' relationship now with Dara is like that of a distant, fond aunt. I am Dara's mother, Tricia is her birthmother. Dara has no confusion with this, any more than she is confused with having two grandpas and grandmas, thirteen cousins and a dozen aunts and uncles. It is just more extended family. I've heard Dara and her friends playing house and when there is a dispute about who gets to be the "Mom" I've heard Dara say, "Okay, I'll be the Mom, and you be the birthmom. You're too young and still in school so you give me your baby." The children have no problem keeping the roles separate.

Now that Dara is five, and can write (with me spelling out the words) she occasionally wants to write to Triica herself. She sends her pictures, collages, paintings (usually rainbows and hearts ala Care Bears!). Her message is often the same, "Tricia, I love you." How her birthmother must treasure those words! I, Dara's mother, treasure them on the pictures and paintings she gives to me.

Tricia writes letters telling her what she is doing. She sends pictures of her cats and herself. Dara noticed she had her hair cut. She wanted to know if she has blue eyes as Dara does.

These two people in my life are establishing a relationship that seems so taken for granted by most of us, that of parent and child. That is their connection, but they must still create their own relationship. Just as I have created, with Dara, our relationship.

I feel that with cooperative adoption, the children have the opportunity to create this very significant relationship early in their lives, instead of waiting twenty-one years and then meeting a stranger with whom they share an intimate connection, but no relationship thus far. I feel this is a great loss to our children, as well as to the birthparents. I feel that by being able to share their childhood and growing years with their birthparents, these children will not only create richer relationships, but a more secure and grounded self-identity for themselves. And they create love.

I affirm Tricias' biological connection with Dara because it is the truth, and because it is so important for DARA. My hope is that she will not experience that silent anquish of feeling unconnected to the human race, of not knowing where she came from. She is our daughter because we have loved and nurtured her from infancy, and we are forever connected by our heartstrings. But she is Tricias' daughter by blood, and I will encourage her to treasure this vital connection.

Jean Gold's Family

Mike's Birthmother and Adoptive Mother light the candles on his birthday cake.

PHOTOS BY BARRY SLOBIN

Changing Two Closed Adoptions Into Cooperative Ones

By Jean Gold

I am a Licensed Clinical Social Worker in private practice and am presently involved in two cooperative adoptions. I will describe each of them separately although they each impact on one another.

I am the birthmother of a twenty-two year old son, Terry, who was adopted independently at birth, and with whom I have been reunited three years. I am also an adoptive mother of a thirteen year old son, Mike, who has been reunited with his birthmother for two years and with his birthfather for one year.

Three years ago, Thanksgiving 1981, my son Terry called me. He had seen a movie *Someone Who Looks Like Me* on television and then joined a search group near his home. Terry had searched for me for approximately two months and by the time he found me, he had a great deal of information. He maintained that he was just curious, and had never asked questions or been interested in his birthfamily. I, on the other hand, was very interested and concerned all through the nineteen years since I had relinquished him. I had joined another search group and was also searching, but was not moving as quickly due largely to being bogged down with guilt and anxiety. Terry had told his adoptive parents that he was searching and they were supportive, although he said that his mother cried when she first heard.

I flew up to see Terry approximately three weeks after he first called. Prior to that we had exchanged several letters, pictures and phone calls. I spent several days in a motel while visiting Terry. We saw the school I had attended, the family home I lived in when he was born, my old boarding house, the hospital where he was born and so on. During that visit Terry's parents invited me over for dinner. We visited, had dinner and I saw where Terry grew up. Things were very pleasant and it was clear that both Terry and I wanted a long-term relationship.

Terry has terrific parents. Ed and Mary have been married for thirty-five years and have lived in the same home for thirty years. They have an adopted daughter, Kelly, two years younger than Terry, and a large extended family. We got along from the beginning and it was clear that we both wanted what is best for Terry.

Since meeting we have spent one week together on vacation (both families) each year. We have gone camping together twice and once our family spent a week at Terry's home over Easter vacation. I have been married for eighteen years and have two other children (Mike, age 13, adopted and Jena, age 9, natural child). Both have flown to visit for a weekend with Terry and his family. We all feel as if Terry's whole family is a part of our extended family and we enjoy our times together.

We have found that we share some activities and interests as families. (E.G. Mike, Ed and Terry like to motorcycle ride. Ed and my husband, Phil like to fish and play cards. Mary and I like to visit. And Jena and Kelly both like to play games). When we are together we are like one "big family". Terry calls his parents "Mom" and "Dad" and Phil and I by our first names. There is no confusion as far as I can tell.

In the begining some of the extended family (aunts and uncles) had some difficulty with this idea of a cooperative adoption. But now that we've all met, things are fine.

My brother has been on several vacations with us and Mary's sister has been on vacation with us. I feel that this form of adoption is the most comfortable possible because there are no secrets and we all respect one another.

My son, Mike (adopted) has been interested in his birthparents all his life. He has always asked who they were, what they looked like, etc. I always told him that if he wished to search we would help him when he was eighteen years old. As I began to get active in the adoption movement, I met many adoptees who talked of their need to know their roots, to see someone who looked like them, and to know who they are. I began to think that perhaps I was being unfair insisting Mike wait until he was eighteen years old. It bothered me to think of his unanswered questions and I wondered how I would feel if I made him wait and then found that one of his parents had died and it was "too late" for answers. I decided that he had the right to know and it would be best for his psychological development if I found his birthparents before he entered his teens.

I searched for several months. During that time I kept a log, and Mike was aware of what was going on in the search most of the time. When we finally found his birthmtoher, Nancy, she was so overwhelmed that she was unable to talk to us on the phone until the next day. Mike spoke to her on the phone and so did I, and then they wrote to one another.

When we found Nancy she was twenty-seven years old, unmarried, had a son, Dustin, three years old and was pregnant. Crystal was born a couple of weeks later. Nancy was living in a mobile home she is purchasing on an acre of land. She was living with her boyfriend and his three children. Several weeks after Crystal was born we drove up to meet Nancy. Mike was so excited. He gave us all instructions as to how to act so we wouldn't embarrass him and announced that no one was to get out of the car until he had met Nancy. It was a joyous and tearful reunion. Nancy truly loves Mike and he loves her. At first all he wanted to do was just be near her and have physical contact. He had loads of questions to ask. We had made up a photo album for her of Mike as he grew up and they looked at it together.

We feel that Mike is a part of his family and they are a part of him. We think of Nancy at times as a daughter. She is twenty-nine now. I am forty-three and my husband is fifty-nine. In fact, my husband has a daughter who is one year older than Nancy.

We try to include Nancy and her family in the holidays. She has met all of Mike's relatives and has stayed over on vacation at our house. We have also been to her home on the holidays and Mike often spends school vacations with her. We all try to keep in mind that each of us has something unique to offer in our relationship with Mike and we are not in competition with one another.

Mike speaks to Nancy on the phone about once a week and occasionally I call her if it has to do with the holidays, etc. Nancy knows what our rules are for Mike and for the most part agrees. At times, she says she would be harder on him than we are.

Naturally, there was a honeymoon period at first when Nancy could do no wrong and we could do no right in Mikes eyes. This period lasted for about six months and then Mike's expectations became more realistic. After Mike had known Nancy for about a year, he began to ask in earnest to meet his father. We searched for his father, Harvey and found him after about six months. Harvey was thrilled to meet Mike even though he had not known of his existance. Harvey and his family were accepting of Mike from the start. Shortly after the meeting we had all of Harvey's extended family over for dinner and to visit. We have stayed in contact with them, and Mike calls his grandparents often.

The reunion with Harvey has not worked out quite as well as with Nancy. Harvey has his own personal problems to work out and there are times that Mike does not hear from him for months and other times when we have to put controls on Mike's visits with Harvey. Despite these problems, I feel the reunion has been worthwhile. Mike has learned about his nationality, what he will probably look like when he is older, and where some of his talents came from. Harvey has his own auto mechanics shop and Mike has always been interested in and done well at mechanics. So now he knows where those abilities come from.

The important issue is that Mike is happy. So many of his questions that we could not answer, have been answered, and he now has a large extended family with many more people to love and care for him.

Bekki and Kristy

PHOTOS BY BARRY SLOBIN

Karen and Kristy

Harry and Karen Kobseff; daughter Kristy; Birthmother, Bekki

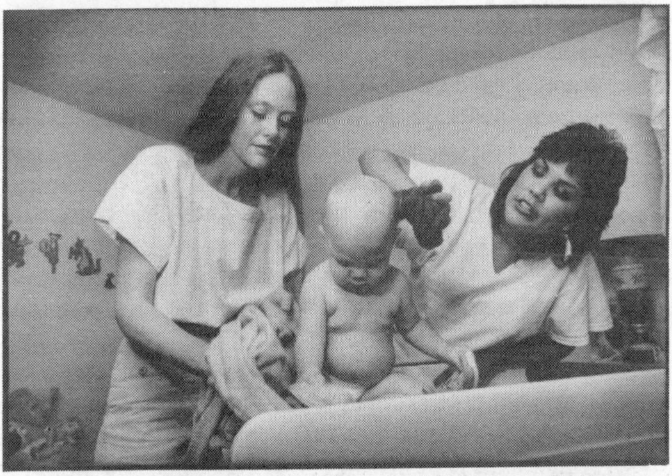

Adoptive Mom, Karen; Kristy; and Birthmom, Bekki

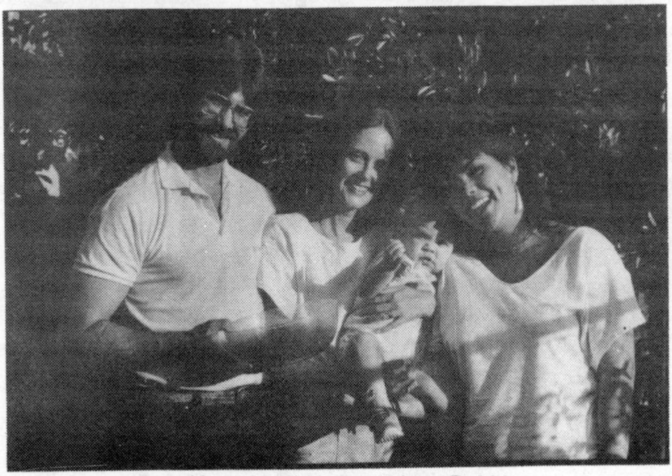

Karen and Harry, Kristy, Bekki

PHOTOS BY BARRY SLOBIN

A Healed Heart and Answered Prayer

By Bekki Saylon

When I first had the feeling I was pregnant I was going through a stage of rebellion. I was very much involved with the punk movement. I didn't care for anybody. I didn't like society. I didn't like the world or how it was working. I was rebelling against my Mom...I was rebelling against everything.

But deep, deep down inside I was crying, I was hurting and I was saying "Will somebody love me?" I don't like the way I feel. I always had a shield over me that nobody could get into. Everybody thought I was happy, fun and so rebellious. I was feeling rotten. I was hiding it all by putting a big smile on my face.

I was dating this older guy, about twenty-two, for quite awhile and I got pregnant. I didn't tell him that I thought I was pregnant. I didn't tell anybody, I just kept it to myself cause I thought how in the world was I going to tell my Mom I was pregnant. I was in a total state of shock, thinking "God, no way, this can't be!" It was an absolute nightmare.

Finally, I got the nerve and told my boyfriend I thought I was pregnant. He was happy. I knew he wasn't going to tell me to get an abortion, he wasn't that type, but his reaction was totally different from what I anticipated. He said "Wow, that's great."

I thought, "You have got to be kidding. That is absolutely crazy. I'm pregnant, I have a baby in my stomach. What am I going to tell my Mom? How am I going to tell my friends, my relatives? What am I going to do?"

I finally told my mom I had a feeling I was pregnant and she was mad and upset like most mothers would be, but she didn't yell at me or threaten to kick me out of the house. Instead of doing that she said this to me, "Becky, regardless of your faults, I still love you and we're going to work together with this." Then she asked, "Why don't you guys get married?" And I thought, oh wow, great, we can get married, that will be cool. I called up my boyfriend and told him that my mom said we could get married and we made all these plans to get married. I was looking at beautiful wedding dresses and cribs for the baby and baby clothes for about a month. I was in school, this was in September and I was two and half months pregnant. My whole family knew and most thought it was good for me to get married. Some of them thought it wasn't good. My friends thought I was crazy but they still accepted me. They still thought of me as their friend. They kept telling me that I should get an abortion or put the baby up for adoption, but whatever I did they'd be on my side.

I didn't know if I was ready to get married, ready to quit going out with my friends, quit dating, quit flirting with other guys and doing all the things a teenager wants to do. I didn't know if I wanted to give up that. I didn't know if I wanted to settle down with one man and raise a baby. I didn't want to drop out of school.

I remember one day, this guy was new at our school, and I thought he was cute. He was punk and I was still in the punk mood—still rebelling. I went out with him once and after that I thought that if I wasn't even married, but planned on getting married, why had I just gone out on my fiance? I cheated on my fiance. I realized I definitely was not ready to get married. If I got married I would regret it because I couldn't date. I would feel deprived of my teenage life. I called up my boyfriend and told him that I didn't want to get married. He was upset and furious at me.

He asked why. I told him I wasn't ready and I didn't want to quit school. Then he asked how I was going to raise the baby by myself, without its father. I told him I'd get an abortion. He said, "You are disgusting. You are crazy. I don't want any woman destroying my child." That was the last time I talked to him.

I planned on getting an abortion and then I realized that I could not kill this baby. It was a life inside of me. I didn't have the guts to do that.

I remember telling my mom I didn't want to get married and she was glad, feeling it would not have been a good idea anyway. So we called off all the plans and I was still going to school. Nobody could really tell that I was pregnant yet 'cause at three or four months I was still really small. I was depressed all the time because I didn't know what to do. I was so confused. I loved my baby and then again I didn't want to have the baby. I just wished I was never pregnant. I wished I was never in that spot.

I was rebelling even worse at times. My mom used to force me to go to church. I hated to go to church. I was a Christian but I backslid so far that I didn't want to face God anymore. I was too guilty. One day my mom forced me to go to church and I sat way in the back of the sanctuary. I didn't want anything to do with God. I remember that some beautiful woman was there for something special. She had a beautiful voice and seemed very sweet. I was in the back and nobody knew how I was feeling. I had locked everybody out of my life and just stuck to myself. There were times when I would cry and cry, not knowing what to do. I used to feel the baby move and kick. It made me laugh, it was so neat, I fell in love with the baby more and more everyday. Everytime it moved I'd fall more in love.

I was just so scared. So frightened of deciding what to do, of wondering what was ahead for me and the baby. Everybody in the church was praying—nobody knew what I was feeling. Then this lady said, "The spirit of God is telling me that there is someone here that has a broken heart. Someone is feeling depressed, confused and God wants to free you from that. If that is you would you come up." I knew that was me. I had tears pouring down my face. I looked at her and she looked at me. I was the only one who got up. I cried. She put her arms around me and loved me and told me, "If you would quit running from God, if you would come back to Him, whatever the problem is, He will mend your heart and guide you in the way you should go. God will see you through this, through his eyes of love." That just cleansed my entire body. It was like the whole depression that was hovering over me vanished. It lifted off my body and I felt so much better. I still cried, but not as bad as before.

I was telling my mom I wanted to put the baby up for adoption. I thought that was the best thing to do. I didn't want to do it but I knew it is the best thing to do. So she told me of this one place and I called a counselor. The counselor told me all the alternatives. I made an appointment, she counseled me and asked me about my feelings. Then she pulled out some files and told me I could look at the couples who wanted to adopt. I looked through and I picked out some families. I remember the first couple I picked lived in a good area. I was thinking that if I was going to give my baby over to some people I wanted them to be rich. I didn't want my child to live in a scungy home or anything like that. So I picked this real wealthy family. I got a chance to talk to them and they were sweet, neat people. I thought I wanted my child to be with these people but deep inside I wasn't really satisfied because the whole time I interviewed them it seemed all they were concerned with was the baby. They didn't seem to care much about me. They didn't seem to like my appearance. By looking at me they could tell I came out of the punk scene. I answered their questions about drugs and beer and told them I was into that up until about the fourth month and they didn't seem very comfortable. I remember coming home after that interview thinking that I wasn't sure if I should choose them. I prayed and said to God, "If that is not the family you want my child to be with then you will shut the doors. You will find a way to bring in another couple that you want the baby to be with." I realized I was being selfish. I was saying I wanted what I want rather than what God wants. Sure enough, I got a call from my counselor and she said that couple did not want to adopt the baby because they were afraid I might change my mind and keep my baby. So I knew that was not the right family and I had to look for some other people.

I was due in about two months. I went to talk to the counselor to look at another file and this time I was ready. She handed me a little piece of paper saying they didn't normally do this but they had just gotten this little letter with a picture of the couple who wanted to adopt. There was no background on them or anything yet, just their written profile. I read it and I liked what I read. I read it again, and again. I really felt satisfied with this couple. Gosh, these people talk about God and that is the way I want my baby to be brought up. In a home where she can be brought up as a Christian. I didn't want my child to go through the drugs or rebellion that I went through. I didn't want my child to be a punk or mingle with alot of punk rockers. Even though I was going through it I didn't want my child to go through it.

I told my counselor that was the family that I wanted. She called them up and told them that I was interested in them and I got a chance to talk to them. The minute they walked in the door I knew deep down in my heart it was them. I knew it! I didn't want to show it but I knew it. I was sad but then again I was happy. I was sad that I was going to give my baby away but I was happy they were going to take care of her. I knew that is what God wanted for me and for the baby.

We talked and talked. They were so concerned about me, even more than about the baby. It seemed that they wanted what I wanted. It made me feel comfortable. They made me feel special and that's what counted the most. When I went home I was crying and told my mom that I knew that was them.

I called the counselor and said those were the people I wanted for my baby. She said okay. I called my ex-boyfriend and told him what I was going to do and he was upset but knew it was the best thing to do. He still loved me like he always did even though I didn't love him any more. He said he was sad but that he knew it was right.

I was due really soon and it really touched my heart when they sent a card that said they were thinking of me. My friends thought I was crazy talking to the people who were going to adopt my baby. I told them we'd arranged monthly pictures and yearly updates after that, and some year I'd see her. They thought that was crazy. They didn't understand. Some of the people I knew at school thought I was terrible for giving up my baby for adoption.

I had the baby. I had real easy labor. I remember saying before she was born that I wanted a girl. When I was in labor I asked my mom to call Harry and Karen (the adopting couple) and said I wanted them to be in the delivery room with me. When they were pushing me in the delivery room I saw Karen and Harry. I could see in Karen's eyes how much she was concerned. My daughter was out within three pushes, and they put her on my stomach. I was amazed... that was my baby! Karen leaned over to me and told me they wanted what I wanted. So I told them I wanted them to go and see her. The doctor asked me if I wanted to see the baby after they cleaned her up and I said no. But I looked at Karen and Harry and said "You go see the baby. It's your baby, you guys go see it."

They said, "But we want what you want Bekki." and I reassured them that I wanted them to see her cause it was their first baby. I wanted this to be as close as possible for them to having a baby. They were really excited about that. Then I fell asleep.

I woke up in my other room and Karen came in with a vase of flowers with a card. We got to talking, it was real special. I was really excited. I was never depressed at the hospital. People told me these big horror stories like if I saw the baby I would cry and not want to give her up for adoption. They told me they wouldn't see the parents if they were me....they wouldn't do this and that. But I felt comfortable with this.

I remember the last day in the hospital when it was time for me to hand the baby over to them I was ready. I was mentally and emotionally ready. I called up my pastor and told him I wanted him to dedicate the baby to them. He was really privileged about that. It was the most beautiful baby dedication ever. I cried and handed the baby over to Karen and Harry looking straight into their eyes telling them what I had to say. I knew this was it. After the dedication was over we talked more and then I went home.

That was the hardest part. I would cry and cry cause she was gone. I felt so empty. I couldn't look at other babies 'cause it made me cry. But I handled it well. It hurt so bad. I told myself that I was going to go through with this, I was not going to take that baby back. I was going to go through with the adoption and that's it!

I went back to school and finished school. Harry and Karen kept their promises. They wrote me letters and sent me pictures and I thought it was the greatest thing in the world for them to send me pictures. I'd get overwhelmed with tears. I love Karen and Harry alot. I love my daughter, Kristy. I never regretted putting her up for adoption 'cause I know it was the best thing to do and I know God will use my daughter in a mighty way. I believe that I will be blessed for giving her life.

I went through the physical pain, the mental pain and the emotional strain and pain all for them and my child. Karen and Harry are the greatest parents. Sure I could have kept my daughter, gone on welfare, dropped out of school, but to me it wouldn't have worked out that way.

I don't know what it means to be a mother. I don't know how to raise a child. That is a massive responsibility and I know Karen is ready to be a mother and Harry is ready to be a father. I know they are going to raise her the right way. Kristy won't be deprived of anything, she'll have everything, she'll have a father. My God, I didn't have a father and I don't want Kristy to go through life without a father. I don't know my father and I wish I did. I know there is going to be a time in life when she will want to see us and when Kristy is ready she will know me. I'm available cause I love my daughter with all my heart. I look at the pictures and I cry cause I miss her so much, but I never regret. I thank God Karen and Harry were there to take Kristy. They are raising her, loving her and giving her everything that I would want to give her.

A Healed Heart and Answered Prayer

By Harry & Karen Kobzeff

We have been blessed with our daughter, Kristy Marie, through a cooperative adoption. We are thrilled about this precious child who has brought so much love, laughter, and happiness into our hearts and home. She is everything and so much more than we ever hoped and dreamed, and we love her more than words could ever express. As we look back over the eight months since her birth, it's hard to believe all that has transpired. We could have never foreseen the depth of feeling and emotion, the overwhelming love and fulfillment, that we have experienced as a result of the openness in our adoption situation. Thus far, it has been a time of growth and learning, about ourselves, the birthparents, and adoption in general. Our traditional concepts of adoption have changed because we have been exposed to and experienced some of what the "other side" goes through.

Although our adoption could be referred to as "independent" or "open" or "cooperative", from the beginning it has been a process of evolving openness, and the relationship with our birthparents, more particularly our birthmother, has grown closer and more comfortable with time. Initially, we didn't feel we could handle an ongoing relationship other than letters and pictures. We wanted openness, but remained conservative and reserved when it came to actually interacting with the birthparents. We wanted time to adjust to and bond with our baby without outside influences.

Our feelings began to change. Because of the birthparents' respect and support of us as Kristy's parents, we have gradually been released from the common apprehensions associated with this type of adoption. We have been concerned about their feelings and have tried to remain open and sensitive to their needs. We have never been able to simply forget they existed. It has given us great joy to know that our daughter's birthparents really like us and truly love her. Their affirmation of us and our ideas in raising Kristy is one more positive link in the chain that makes up our adoption experience. Every year new links will be added, until it stretches a lifetime, and our sincere and heartfelt prayer is that ALL the lives that are touched through this process will be enriched and blessed.

Our adoption came about after three years of trying to have a baby with no success. We spent one year in infertility testing and as a result began to consider adoption. Our testing was inconclusive, surgery showed everything as it should be, and the cause of our not conceiving still a mystery. Because we are in our early thirties we felt it was time to begin checking with some adoption agencies. I began in the yellow pages, looking for every source possible that might have an adoption service or know of one. We also spoke with a ministry affiliated with our church that has an outreach to birthmothers, as well as talked to friends and family who might be able to give us suggestions. Most importantly, we began to pray. We knew that the Lord had, and has, our best interests at heart. We looked to Him to guide us in our desire for a child.

Some special friends began to pursue adoption through independent means and asked if I could help in typing their biographical letter. This started the wheels turning in our minds that maybe an "independent" adoption might be for us.

The adoption situations that were referred to us all seemed uncomfortable in one way or another. One situation we felt good about fell through because another couple was chosen. In another case, the counselor wanted an unreasonable amount of money to be flown down to interview families for the birthmother. There were too many uncertainties. Another woman was wavering in her decision, and although she had chosen us, she decided to go through an agency because she didn't trust herself not to take the baby back. We admired her honesty and consideration of us. At this point the stress was overwhelming. Hundreds of dollars had been spent on attorneys. The timing wasn't right. We still had to work through our feelings about adoption and what we could really handle. I had more trouble than Harry in this area. From the time I was a little girl, I knew I wanted to adopt a child or children when I grew up. But I never thought it would be my ONLY alternative in having a baby. I didn't know if I would feel close to an adopted child ... like it was really my own. Would I feel like a foster parent or babysitter? Would I be able to love the child with *all* my heart? Could I handle the openness required in an "independent" adoption? I needed more time to deal with this. I had not had surgery yet and we felt that we should at least rule out any physical problems before we actively pursued adoption.

Once the surgery was over, we felt a burden lifted from our shoulders and began again to discuss adoption. This time I was ready, anticipating the arrival of a baby into our home. I had worked through the personal feelings about myself and adoption by now. Harry and I were both excited about contacting the church ministry and sending our letter and picture to them first. They maintain files of prospective adoptive couples that birthmothers can choose from. There is no numbering system, no waiting list. The ministry encourages the birthmothers to meet the couple they have chosen.

Our letter was sent February 18, 1984. Two weeks later, Harry received a phone call at work from one of the counselors. A young woman had seen our letter and wanted to meet us. She would be interviewing another couple and making her final decision. They added that it was highly unusual for us to be chosen so soon—they had no file set up on us yet. Our letter had been on the counselor's desk when the birthmother came in for a counseling appointment. She had seen it on the desk and asked to review it. Consequently, a meeting was set up for two weeks later.

At this point we were excited...wondering...yet at peace, comfortable taking things one step at a time. Our concern was not only that we be blessed with a baby, but that the birthmother feel secure in her decision. Wanting a child can become an all-consuming desire, overshadowing every area of a person's life. At times the pain and yearning for a baby seemed to overpower me. I prayed that God would strengthen me as a woman, with or without a child, and give me complete peace and joy first — BEFORE I was blessed with a baby. I wanted to be content and whole right where I was at. Only then could I offer a chld the best that I could give. How thankful I am that He did just that! We went to the meeting desiring to be used in this young woman's life as an encouragement to her, maybe even a vehicle to enlighten her as to what prospective adoptive couples feel and go through, to help her in her final decision. If we weren't chosen, then we knew with all certainty that this was not the right situation for us. We wanted this young woman to make her decision independent of outside opinions and pressures, and solely from her heart. We wanted her to know that we wanted not only what was best for the child, but also for her.

We were the second of two couples being interviewed that evening by the birthmother, Bekki, and her mother. Their primary concern was that the child be raised in a strong Christian home. She asked us questions, we asked her questions. After an hour of talking, the interview ended. We waited outside while our counselor talked with mother and daughter. We wondered what they thought of us, how we were perceived.

Well.... we were chosen that night! We spent another two hours talking with the counselor afterward and then began the waiting game. At this point we were informed that the birthparents were on good terms but there was no ongoing relationship between them. We were told that the birthfather was supportive of Bekki's decision regarding the adoption.

The delivery due date was supposedly five weeks away. It was all happening so fast! We did not meet Bekki again prior to the birth, but were in contact through our counselor at the church. We were informed that she would like us to be present in the delivery room when the baby was born, to bond with him or her immediately and to experience everything we could right from the beginning. We were thrilled, yet wondering what this would be like. We hadn't gotten to know Bekki too well yet. We didn't have the benefit of months to bond or going to prepared childbirth classes with her, but our counselor was her coach and kept us abreast of what to do. Harry and I realized that we were already bonding in our hearts with our unborn baby. It was a beautiful process and one that is difficult to put into words. We had previously planned a ski trip out of state just prior to the baby's birth and when we returned we had a week and a half to get the house ready before the approximate delivery date. Then the phone call came! It was Sunday,

April 22, 1984, about 4:30 a.m. and our counselor was heading for the hospital. Bekki had been admitted in the early morning hours. We were told not to rush...it would be *at least* noon or so before she deliverd. The counselor suggested we come to the hospital about 7:00 or 7:30 am. It was Easter morning!

At 6:55 a.m., just as we were about to walk out the door, the phone rang again. This time it was Bekki's mother saying we'd better get to the hospital quick! Well, we flew down the freeway and arrived in record time! We didn't know where to go but found our way to the waiting area. In the room across the hall we could hear the cries and moans of a woman in labor. The panting ... then the rest periods ... then again the cry of pain. It was *our* birthmother. It was *our* baby pushing it's way into the world! We realized the self sacrifice, the physical pain that Bekki was going through to give this child life. I thought of the emotional and physical loss she would experience in placing that child with us ... I couldn't hold back the tears. My heart ached for her. All my fears of the birthmother vanished. My heart went out to her and I wanted to let her know how much we admired and loved her for what she was doing.

The next thing we knew, we were dressing in "moon suits" (as Harry calls them) to go into the delivery room. The room was warm and peaceful, yet we were anxious, awaiting the arrival of this precious child. The doctor finally came. It was 7:45 a.m. and three pushes later our baby was born...a beautiful, healthy little girl!

We will all never forget how white she was... the cord being cut... her first cry. We were in awe. She was so big and so alive! Bekki insisted that we stay with the baby and go into the nursery to experience all the "firsts" immediately after birth. This meant so much to us. We spent the next few hours watching the nurses swaddle and check our baby and do all the tests they do right after birth.

That Easter Sunday, the first day of Kristy's life outside the womb, was quite an eventful one. We were at the hospital off and on all day. We were encouraged to bond with Kristy and feed her. The hospital staff were so open and supportive to us as an adoptive couple, and to the birthparents. They taught us how to do everything. They even had a woman on call who would come to our home during the first weeks after birth to show us how to give baths, etc. We tried not to overstep our bounds and to remain enough in the background to give the birthparents time to adjust and make this decision without pressure from us. We were right there, involved in everything, but not demanding anything of our birthmother or the hospital. When decisions were necessary and we were asked, we decisively made those decisions. We never wanted to appear to be taking over, but rather working together with the birthparents. It was a bittersweet time of joy and sorrow. Such a delicate balance.

That evening while we were visiting Kristy, her birthfather, Bruce, came to the hospital to see her for the first time. This was something we did not expect. So when the nurse informed us that he was there, we weren't sure what to do. The nurse pointed him out at the nursery window. We looked over at him gazing at Kristy in her bassinet, tears were streaming down his face. Our hearts broke. We were so happy about Kristy being a part of our lives, yet our hearts were grieving with this man. We wanted him to know that we cared. As it turned out, he came back later while we were feeding Kristy and we had an opportunity to meet him face to face. He knew about us from Bekki. He was very kind and sensitive to us, even asking if it was alright for him to hold the baby. We stepped back, giving him time with her. We didn't feel threatened. We realized we had no rights yet as adopting parents—the birthparents had every right to do as they wished. We wanted Bruce to know that we weren't pushing him aside. Meeting him was a very positive thing for us. It's easy to assume and make mental pictures about someone you've never met. The reality of who Bruce was eased our fears and preconceived ideas about this person in the shadows called the *birthfather*. We took a picture of him holding Kristy for the first time. You could see the love he had for her. It was a deeply meaningful experience for us, and we believe for him too. He was also able to see who these people were that were taking his daughter to be their own. And he wished us all the best. In the midst of his pain he was thinking of us. We told him we were sending Bekki pictures and progress reports as the baby grew and asked if he would like them too...Yes!...he'd love them!

The next day I returned to the hospital and had the priviledge of visiting Bekki in her room. It was a special time... just woman to woman. It meant alot to me to have that time with her. I didn't really know what to say. What do you say to a woman who has just given birth to a baby and given that baby to you to raise? I tried to be sensitive and let her know we cared about her. We discussed baby names, things she was going to do, and then she gave me a stuffed lamb (named Lammy!) to give the baby. Again, my heart was filled to overflowing.

Bekki has always been sensitive to us as the adoptive couple. She shared her preference in baby names but left the final decision up to us. We wanted to do the right thing—for the baby, the birthparents, and ourselves. We realized there was an extended family involved with "our child", and there were additional considerations.

The day for Bekki to leave the hospital came, two days after the birth. It seemed like weeks had passed ... so much had happened! She had requested that her pastor and his wife, her mother, our counselor, ourselves, she and Kristy be present when she left. She wanted to have a dedication ceremony for Kristy. So, in one of the empty labor rooms, with doors closed, we all began to share together, talking about how God had put us together and how special our situation was. Bekki prayed, acknowledging she knew this was God's will, and she personally gave me the baby, placing her in my arms and acknowledging us as Kristy's parents. The pastor prayed for us as a family and for Bekki. We prayed for Bekki as well. We all were crying, arms around each other. Pictures were taken. God was doing beautiful work.

Bekki left the room shortly after. I'll never forget the look on her face...the longing, the pain, that glance back over her shoulder, and then the look downward as she walked out the door. Again my heart was aching for her. How much she had gone through at seventeen.

At three days old Kristy left the hospital and came home with us. The first few months we communicated via the church ministry. We all were aware of each other's addresses but because our communication was limited before the baby's birth and because we didn't know just how much the birthparents could handle or how much we felt comfortable with, we kept the church as liaison for a time. Bekki surprised me with a Mother's Day card and Harry with a Father's Day card along with letters. That was more special than words could ever express. It was a tremendous encouragement. Bekki had been quiet and not very talkative with us prior to the birth. We didn't really know how she felt about us. We knew she must have liked something but we felt some distance between us. We knew we wanted a meaningful relationship with her. After about four months, Harry and I began discussing the possibility of writing directly to Bekki and not going through the church. It seemed like a comfortable thing to do but we didn't know what Bekki would think. It was taking twice as long for her to receive things from us with the "middleman". Of course, the same was true for Bruce.

Seven months after Kristy's birth, Bekki, her mother and sister came to our home for dinner. And yes... Kristy was there! It was a beautiful experience for all of us. No fears, no uneasiness, no tension. I had wondered if I would feel left out, like an outsider, when Kristy was with her natural family, knowing that I didn't give birth to her. We know we are her mommy and daddy and are confident in that role. Kristy's birthfamily supports us in our role as parents. This is why we can feel comfortable and not threatened by the natural family. Our common Christian faith is the bond that ties us all so closely together.

It was like no time had passed since seeing them last at the hospital. They have become like family to us. Kristy belongs to all of us and all of us belong to her. We talked and talked, ate, and took pictures. We learned so much about Bekki and what she went through before the birth of our daughter. They asked if it would be alright to see us again before Christmas to give Kristy presents, and we said of course! So, they had us for dinner and we had a wonderful time getting better acquainted, praying together, laughing and sharing our love for one precious little girl. This time Bruce was there too.

Bekki said that one of the things that helped her decide on us as parents was that we were interested not only in the baby, but also in her. She needed to know we weren't going to "take the baby and run", even though we didn't anticipate physical contact with her after the birth ... at least not for some time. She shared with us that in talking with Bruce he said he liked us because, "At least they care about us, too."

On December 28, 1984, our adoption was finalized in court. We feel fortunate to have been able to meet both birthparents and to be able to get to know them a little more as time goes by. It has touched our hearts and expanded our understanding of a very complex life-changing situation. At this point we are open to a continuing relationship with both birthparents. We don't know what will happen in the future or how we will feel. Nor do we know how we will handle all the issues surrounding the raising of our daughter, Kristy. As time goes on, needs may change and we will flow with all our changing needs. Our main concern is the well-being of Kristy—what she can handle and what's best for her. We have many issues to discuss and work through as she grows up. The important thing for us is that all of this will serve to enrich Kristy's life, self-concept, identity, and overall well-being.

Appendix

**We Have Two Mommies,* a full length book of the concepts learned in one families cooperative adoption is pending publication. For information write to: Nita Jo Frees, 1223 Tico Road, Ojai, CA 93023.

There are Cooperative Adoption Support Group meetings and audio tapes available from Parenting Resources, 250 El Camino Real, Suite 111, Tustin, CA 92680.

Referrals to facilitators and families, the Introductory Cooperative Adoption Package, and audio and video tapes are available from TRIADOPTION Library, Inc. Box 638, Westminster, CA 92684.

SAMPLE	TYPE OF LETTER OR EXAMPLE	PAGE
A	Attorney/Client Agreement	89
B	Medical Records Request	91
C	Hospital/Medical Records Release Agreement	92
D	State/Agency Files Release Form	93
E	State/Agency Files Release Agreement	94
F	Hospital Release	96
G	Authorization For Pick Up Of Child	97
H	Petition To Adopt	98
I	Consent To Adopt	99
J	Surrender/Relinquishment	100
K	Final Decree	101-2
L	Original Birth Certificate Request Letter	103
M	Original Birth Certificate	104
N	Amended Birth Certificate — Unpreferrable	105
O	Adoption Certificate — Preferrable	106

Informative Reading

ADOPTION

ADOPTION—Current Issues and Trends by Paul Sachev. 1983, Butterworths, $39.95.
"A practicitioners guide to sound practice in administration and professional adoption service."

THE ADOPTION SEARCHBOOK: Techniques For Tracing People by Mary Jo Rillera, 1981. Triadoption Publications, Box 5218, Huntington Beach, CA 92646 $15.00.
"A complete guide and manual for all separated families wanting to search for information or missing family members."

THE ADOPTION TRIANGLE by Sorosky, Baran and Pannor, 1978. Anchor Press, $3.95.
"Detailed research compiled over five years on all sides of the triad. Portions of letters received in this in-depth study."

ADOPTION, THE GRAFTED TREE by Laurie and William Wishard. Avon Books, Cragmont Publications, China Basis Bldg. 161 Berry St. #6410, San Francisco, CA 94107 $3.50.

ADOPTIVE KINSHIP by H. David Kirk (A Modern Institution in Need of Reform). 1981, Ben-Simon Publications, Box 867, Waterloo, Canada $11.95.
"A look at the institution and its social impact and potential growth."

AN ADOPTER'S ADVOCATE, by Patricial Irwin Johnston, 1984. Perspectives Press, 905 W. Wildwood Ave., Ft. Wayne, IN 46805.
General Information Book.

THE ART OF ADOPTION by Linda Cannon Burgess, 1976, Acropolis Books, 2400 17th St. NW. Washington, DC 20009. Hdcvr $8.95.
"A social workers look at the 900 adoptions she was responsible for during her career and the effects reviewed on those families years later."

THE BABY BROKERS by Lynne McTaggert, 1979. Dial Press, 1 Dag Hammarskjold Plaza, New York, NY 10017, Hdcvr. $10.95.
"The marketing of white babies in America."

THE BABY CHASE by Tony Korheiser, 1983. Atheneum, New York,$12.95.
"A true story of confrontation with infertility, adoption and 'grey market' baby 'selling.'"

BEATING THE ADOPTION GAME by Cynthia D. Martin, 1980. Oak tree Publications, Box 1012, La Jolla, CA 92038, $9.95.
"Looks at who controls adoption, how to beat the system and how to reform it."

THE BEREAVED PARENT by Harriet Sarnoff Schoff. Penguin Books, 625 Madison Av., New York, NY 10022.
"Sensitive sharing of personal loss of a son in an accidental death and the mutual learning that has helped others deal with grief."

BIRTHMARK by Lorraine Dusky, 1979. M. Evans & Co., 216 E. 49th St., New York, NY 10017.
"A birthmother's honest story of pregnancy, surrender and after."

CHOICES, CHANCES, CHANGES A booklet compiled by Concerned United Birthparents, 595 Central Ave. Dover, NH, $5.00.
"A guide to making an informed choice about an untimely pregnancy—a must for all parents considering adoption."

DEAR BIRTHMOTHER by Kathleen Silber and Phyllis Speedlin, 1982. Adoption Awareness Press, 4703 Paradise Woods, San Antonio, TX 78249.
"Proceedures and experiences of open adoptions."

DEATH BY ADOPTION by Joss Shawyer, 1979. Cicada Press, Box 64-009, Birkenhead South, Aukland, 10, New Zealand.
"Account of tactics used by society to swindle women out of their 'unwanted' children."

HOW IT FEELS TO BE ADOPTED by Jill Krementz, 1982. Alfred A. Knopf, New York, NY, $11.95.
"Nineteen boys and girls from eight to sixteen share their feelings—includes photos."

I'M STILL ME by Betty Jean Lifton, 1981. Alfred A. Knopf, 201 E. 50th, New York, NY 10022, $8.95.
"Wonderful story of a teenager in search. A good teen novel."

IN SEARCH OF ORIGINS by John Triseliotis, 1975. Beacon Press.
"Study of the adoptions and adoptees in England."

I WOULD HAVE SEARCHED FOREVER by Sandra Kay Musser, 1979. Jan Enterprises, Box 268, Bala Cynwyd, PA 19009. Ppbk $4.50.
"The first book by a birthparent about her own experience and faith."

JODY by Jerry Hulse, 1976. McGraw Hill.
"True story of the search for his wife's birth family in the wake of a life or death operation and the discovery of a twin."

LOST AND FOUND: The Adoption Experience by Betty Jean Lifton, 1979. Dial Press, 1 Dag Hammarskjold Plaza, New York, NY 10017.
"A journey in search and reunion concentrating on those moments of intense awareness when adoptees are tapping their pain."

MOTHER, MOTHER by James Stingley, 1981. Congeon & Lappef, Inc. Empire State Building, New York, NY 10001, $12.95.
"The true story of the dark secret of his past, quest for emotional survival as he confronts and trys to understand his two mothers."

ONE AGAINST THE STORM by Stanley C. Mann, 1980. Quest Publishing, Box 27317, Salt lake City, UT 84127, $6.95.
"True story of an adoptive mother's death, adoptive father's coersion and the guardian's search for the adoptees birthfamily."

OPEN ADOPTION—OPEN PLACEMENT by January Roberts and Diane Robie. Adoption Press, Box 29617, Brooklyn Ctr, MN 55429, $3.95.
"A pocket book looking at open adoption."

ORPHAN TRAIN by James Magnuson & Dorothea G. Petrie, 1978. Fawcett Crest, New York, NY.
"Story compiled with threads of the actual lives of those children carried cross-country to homes in the west."

THE SECRET LIFE OF THE UNBORN CHILD by Thomas Verny, 1981. Delta Books, Dell Publ. 1 Dag Hammarskjold Plaza, NY 10017.
"A look at pre and perinatal life."

SHARED FATE by David H. Kirk, 1964. Free Press, New York.
"Mr. Kirk is an adoptive father who sensitively handles adoption. —This book was before it's time!"

SO YOU'RE ADOPTED by Fred Powledge, 1982. Charles Scribner's Sons, New York.
"A book for adopted young people about being adopted—anything they feel is OKAY!"

SUCCESSFUL ADOPTION Helen Hornor Plumez, 1982. Harmony Books, Crown, One Park Av., New York 10016, $14.95.
"A guide to finding and raising an adoptive family."

A TIME FOR SEARCH by Henry Ehrlich, 1977. Paddington Press.
"Collection of stories gathered from interviews with members of the triad."

TO LOVE AND LET GO by Suzanne Arms, 1984. Knopf, $14.95.
"Shows more than one way for adoptions to be handled. Birthparents can choose adoptive families and bypass the lengthy agency process."

UNDERSTANDING THE BIRTHPARENT edited by Lee Campbell, CUB, 595 Central Av, Dover, NH $5.00.
"Twenty-five birthmothers tell their stories concisely and honestly."

WHICH MOTHER IS MINE? by Joan Oppenheimer, 1980. Bantam Books, 666 5th Av., New York, NY 10019, Ppbk.
"A teenager is confronted with the return of her birthmother just as her foster family wants to adopt her."

The Authors...

MARY JO RILLERA, adoptee and birthparent involved in adoptions that have changed from closed to cooperative; author of *The Adoption Searchbook*, national speaker and consultant on family separation and continuity; Guardian Trustee International Soundex Reunion Registry; Founder TRIADOPTION Library, Inc., P.O. Box 638, Westminster, CA 92684.

PHOTO BY RON REGEV

SHARON KAPLAN, adoptive parent involved in cooperative adoptions; social worker for twenty-five years working with birth and adoptive families; national lecturer on adoption issues; member of Board of Trustees TRIADOPTION Library, Inc.; Director of Parenting Resources, 250 El Camino Real, Suite 111, Tustin, CA 92680.